St. Lou-isms

Lingo, Lore, and the Lighter Side of Life in the Gateway City

John L. Oldani, PhD

REEDY PRESS
St. Louis, Missouri

This one's for

Gemma, Josie, Ceci
Charlie, Gianna

Who for the last eight years have informed everything that I have done or tried to do.

I hope I will make you proud.

Reedy Press
PO Box 5131
St. Louis, MO 63139, USA
www.reedypress.com

Library of Congress Control Number: 2013934330

ISBN: 978-1-935806-44-8

For more information, visit www.stlouisfolklore.com.

Design by Jill Halpin

Printed in the United States of America
13 14 15 16 17   5 4 3 2 1

Contents

This is your 15 minutes; get over it!

Acknowledgments

For some readers the Acknowledgments section borders on cliché. Every author thanks everyone he has met in his lifetime! Not sincere, they carp! Well, let the critics roar. I do want to thank everyone who has been part of my life. It's the nature of folklore fieldwork to be aware, questioning, inquisitive, doubtful, probing, and even obnoxious. I have had hundreds—no thousands—of informants who have given me their lore. And I have been touched by all of them. They may not have realized that they were validating or speaking lore, but they are part of what I have documented in this research. I sincerely thank all of my informants for the examples of their folkways. Collected and combined, they allowed for a definition of a St. Louis culture.

There are some informants, however, who helped me edit, suggested themes, and talked me through my thousands of folk texts. Most of the time my excitement at what I had collected was undoubtedly boring to them, but they patiently listened and I documented. In a pure sense, not a cliché, this research could not have been completed without their support.

To Janet Huenke, who "gets it," a special thanks for her applied bantering, delightful sarcasm, and a "no-holds-barred" friendship. Bob Corbett, the "mayor" of Dogtown, was generous with his time and research and was enthusiastic about my fieldwork. We had commonality as fellow "Micks," and I took obscene advantage of the connection. No one knows "Irish" better than Bob. In his friendship I am happily O'Danny! To Jim Dowd III, who, again, brainstormed with me many times, introduced me to informants, tweaked my themes, and suggested excellent secondary sources for validation. He is a treasured friend. To Marion Cawl Covington, a "younger" friend, as she reminds me, of long standing, who was always available to compare and confirm her family experiences with the lore I had collected. She served as my generous personal expert who provided lore with different and excellent variations. A special thank you to Azim Mujakic, my good Bosnian friend, without whom the lore of the St. Louis Bosnians could not have been collected. His insights, based on his own dramatic experiences, described the Bosnian experiences of coming to St. Louis as no written document could have. Jim Owens, a friend of long standing, spent hours with me, and in brogue, helped me understand the lore of the Irish. He is a treasured source.

Sincere thanks to Micki Bisesi, my sister, for acting as my agent throughout and knowingly, and more often unknowingly, sparking my brain. To Tom Unwin, Professor Doug McKay, Dr. Steve and Barbara Landay, John Mueller, Don (Pancho) Deachan, Kathy Lass, Cathy Bono Mahoney, Charlie Robinson, Nancy Feeney, Larry Willard, Bill Lemp, John Corbett, and Lou L'Hote, a natural raconteur, for their folklore texts, stories, grasp of the nature of fieldwork, and a real interest in preserving lore. I am very grateful for your contributions. You will recognize your lore in the examples. To Jennifer Meyer Oldani, for caring, asking, and collecting, a big thanks. Carollee, my wife; my three kids Matt, Susan Oldani Hendrickson, and David; and their spouses, Jennifer, Joe, and Monica, have always been my foundation and understood my basic need to record what could be lost forever. You guys have inspired all my research. Thanks for your edits, arguments, and distance when I needed it.

Lastly, and not in the clichéd "least," a genuine and heartfelt thanks to Josh Stevens and Matt Heidenry of Reedy Press. Their discussions, editing, suggestions, creativity, and patience with my advanced ego made this book happen. Matt and Josh are a class act, rare among their peers, and it is my good fortune to have them as publishers, editors, and friends. More than once, I know I must have caused them to rethink their profession! Fortunately, donuts can solve all problems and serve as an inexpensive referee.

Now, read about your lore that connects your past and your present. Pass it on! Give your folk a sense of understanding of who they are. Meet your grandparents and parents again. Better: Find out who you are.

Peace!

Dr. Jack

Introduction

Some insist on the proper name, St. Louis. And a few of them demand Saint Louis. Historians might call it the Gateway to the West. Then a few "in-crowd" accepted Gateway City. No, others argued, it's Mound City, honoring Native Americans. Jazzy, hip residents prefer "St. Louie" reduced in a "cool" utterance to The Lou! Then, there's River City for the landed community. Tweets call it STL. In athletic terms, it's elevated to a larger geographic entity, Cardinal Nation. Some elite call it Hoosier City. How about Arch City? Foodies might call it Concrete City. There's also Blues City. Intellectuals and those of an esoteric bent call it Bunny City referring to the "thinking bunny" sculpture on the campus of Washington University. But all names refer to the city established in 1764, named for King Louis IX of France, that sits on the west bank of the Mississippi River and is universally and fondly depicted in popular culture with the phrase: Meet me in St. Louie, Louie.

There is a commonality, however. The lore of the St. Louis region, identified with the different folk groups, is integrated neatly to define a culture. There are obvious characteristics and patterns in the folk vocabulary, folk grammar and pronunciation, folk beliefs, traditions, rituals, jokes, ethnicities, and even legends in and about St. Louis. When considered as one, the lore reveals a "St. Louis character" which highlights and underscores the true personality of the culture.

In two earlier volumes, *Passing It On: Folklore of St. Louis* and the revised edition of the same book, I attempted to apply the study and science of folklore through fieldwork in the greater St. Louis metropolitan area. From the more than 100,000 folk texts

I collected from informants, it became apparent that folkways unique to St. Louis were being transmitted. Most informants, not surprisingly, were not aware of their own lore and its place in their personal or community life. But the oral traditions were always there, latent but powerful.

The study grew. The folk was identified from the first research documenting language, superstitions, jokes, folk foods, momisms, folk games, autograph book verses, even graffiti, among other folklore, common to St. Louis. They saw reflections of their own maturation and remembered. And they passed it on!

St. Lou-isms is, in many ways, also a study of the folk mores of the St. Louis area. This volume, however, emphasizes the dynamism of folklore. As stated many times, there is not a vacuum in lore. It exists for a reason. Wholly new folk groups are documented with their lore that creates the bond they need. Their manner of speech or pronunciation or catch phrases or jokes or games are vital to their identity. In some cases, the lore is the reason for their development as a folk group.

The "lingo" of St. Louis, for example, collected from eager informants is easily recognized in folk groups and quickly learned and passed on by others. It will be noted that some of the most often used expressions are variants of popular culture or staples of the St. Louis culture. The twist, of course, comes from the folk. How many "pick-up lines" did you know before the folk educated you? Is there really a St. Louis way of saying someone is stupid? These are not the proverbial "old-wives" tales, they are current lore used in daily conversation.

Did your grandparents ever tell you tales about the "Choking Doberman" in the St. Louis area? Or legends about zombies in Wildwood or Florissant? Probably not, but the new lore confirms their existence! And do St. Louis tanning beds really burn from the inside out? Remember the girl with the bee hive hair-do? She still lives in St. Louis tales! So does the ghostly hitchhiker and the scamming grandmother. They are examples of the new lore that defines the area, and the variants are legion.

The new St. Lou-isms also describes how to handle stress, the culture of athletics, the welfare system, and even our educational and religious systems. And it does not forget techies, computers, and all St. Louis "nerds." The folk have ways of defining, complaining about, or identifying the novelties of our culture in the information age. There is purpose and meaning in the current transmission.

The new folklore, also, considers a folk group growing larger every day: senior citizens. Demographic changes caused by baby boomers are clearly identified in their folklore. They will be heard! But the lore collected from seniors is especially important as it is a combination of their nostalgic memories and their clashes with the current folk groups. A lighter side to St. Louis lore is revealed but there is certainly a truth in the parodies.

The proverbial "battle" of the sexes is not lost in the new lore, either. In fact, in St. Louis it takes on a whole new dimension. Is it a response to feminism? To early retirement of men? To more blonde or Dagwood jokes? To the computer? To the glass ceiling? Again, there is a joking culture around and about male vs. female in the new St. Louis lore, but what is really being said?

Occupations and the lore that identifies them are also documented in *St. Lou-isms*. Nurses, lawyers, and athletes are singled out for their seemingly "private" but conspicuously "public" folk texts. The vocabulary, traditions, jokes (from and about each group!), superstitions, rituals, and graffiti are transmitted to bond each group, but the "outside" folk use the transmission in different ways to create a whole new perspective.

Two ethnic groups, chronologically at the opposite ends of immigration in St. Louis, the Irish and Bosnians, are included in this new research and identified through their lore. Both groups have or had a desire to be seen as "St. Louis Americans," but their folkways could not be stifled. In a pure manner, the lore of the "green" and the culture of "sarma" merged with the traditions of St. Louis and developed a larger and more interesting lore. There is truly a St. Louis folk culture of acceptance obvious in the examples of their folklore.

But before you get to the entire lingo, legends, and lighter side of St. Louis lore, let me briefly explain, again, what is meant by folklore.

So what is folklore exactly? First, it is oral in its transmission. One person tells another, then that person tells another, and so on. The joke, the expression, or the ritual becomes a custom. And no one really knows where it started. So anonymity is another criterion. In attempting to understand the world, all folk groups learn to explain occurrences or rationalize events.

A third criterion is that the lore is always passed along in a traditional way. For example, young girls have been jumping rope on grade-school playgrounds for decades and jump rope is still very popular. But the verses of 2013 are far different from the verses of 1950. None of the rhymes were learned in a formal educational setting, but rather by tradition. Always the themes are important to the girls doing the jumping and reflect their concerns about life which they don't fully understand. Jumping and chanting in a prescribed cadence add a sense of play.

Often, the same folk expression, saying, or verse is found in another region, and a fourth criterion, the existence of different versions, suggests even more strongly the need to express oneself exactly as the immediate culture demands. For example, someone in one region might believe that a black cat crossing his or her path is bad luck. Someone in another area knows the same belief but has learned that spitting in the direction of the black cat and then continuing neutralizes the bad luck. Little does the second person know that his belief goes back to the ancients, who thought that spitting sends our "soul spirits" to create good luck.

The belief continues—again, without formal education—but the practice is repeated over and over again. Black cats, as symbols of bad luck, are the theme; the belief is still there, but the optimism of some Americans can convert that bad luck. And observers of the American character have often said that optimism defines us. Found in the folk texts? Absolutely!

St. Louis is one of those regions with a distinct lore. What serves as the basic folklore examples heard and used in the area may be heard in all parts of the country and even elsewhere in the world. But the spin on the folk text and its delivery become characteristically St. Louis's.

Every one of us has been touched by lore. It is integral to our personality and our world view. It serves as our history, our past, our future, our fears, our triumphs, our maturation, our generational ages, our very character.

Folklore can be a chance to reconnect with our grandparents, parents, and siblings to relive our traditions or family history; to understand our contemporaries or colleagues better; and to make connections in this age of very complex changes.

I have been aware of the many forms of folklore and studied them for more than thirty years, and I hear and see new things every day. Folklore has helped explain my world for decades.

Say hello to yourself in each of the succeeding chapters, which are by no means exhaustive. I hope you will recognize where you were, what you were doing, why you did it, and why you still do it when you heard them or spoke the lingo. I hope you will learn some new lore to help explain this complex, changing world. And I hope, most of all, that you continue your traditional lore. It's the one treasure that must not be lost in our "throwaway" society.

Consider this example of the new lore. It's not exclusively a reflection of St. Louis lingo and lore, but its tone sets the theme for a lighter world view. And it has been passed around many times as "solutions" to our "problems." Themes of "annoying self-help," "psychobabble," "sexual conflict," "instant experts and expertise," "work stress," "obvious instructions," and a "plea for common sense" in this rapidly changing, complex, over-indulgent world are all apparent in the following "rules."

SEVEN TO SURVIVE: THE ONLY RULES YOU NEED (PLUS MEDITATION)

1. Avoid cutting yourself when slicing vegetables by getting someone else to hold the vegetable while you chop.

2. Avoid arguments with women about lifting the toilet seat by using the sink.

3. If you have high blood pressure, simply cut yourself and bleed for a few minutes. You will reduce pressure on your veins. But remember to set the timer.

4. Place a cocked mousetrap on top of your alarm clock. This will prevent you from going back to sleep after you hit the snooze button.

5. For a bad cough, take a large dose of laxatives. You'll eventually be afraid to cough.

6. Remember, you need only two tools in life: WD-40 and Duct Tape. If it doesn't move and should, use the WD-40. If it shouldn't move and does, use the tape.

7. If you can't fix it with a hammer, you've got an electrical problem.

Meditate each day: Some people are like Slinkies . . . not really good for anything but they bring a smile to your face when they're pushed down the steps.

Simple rules, but they are not absolute! What's your social issue? Relationships? Technology? Stupidity? Jargon? Men? Women? Seniors? Athletes? Nurses? Lawyers? Hoosiers? Read on and reflect. It's your lingo and lore.

CHAPTER 1

St. Louis Lingo

Okay, is it sodie, soda, pop, or simply coke? Do you sit on a davenport, sofa, divan, or couch? Is it a donut or a cruller? Is it cottage cheese or clabber cheese? Is it Highway Forty or Farty? Do you live in Missour-ee or Missour-ah? Do you "warsh," "worsh," or "woosh" dishes in the "zink"? Do you "rinsh" them? Do you have an "ice box," "refrigerator," or "Frigidaire"?

Folk speech is the simplest level of folklore studies. It can be a word, saying, name, or usage in any particular folk group or folk region. Often these words occur in grammar, pronunciation, and vocabulary and reflect the social folk dialects of a group. Folklorists look to these dialects and speech patterns as they occur in collected folk texts such as sayings, tales, legends, beliefs, superstitions, jokes, families, and even occupational groups. Sometimes the vocabulary of the folk, in all forms and contexts, becomes standard for a region and helps define its culture.

Documenting the folk vocabulary or folk speech of an area, folklorists want to know: Do some forms of folk speech survive in traditional lore? How are they transmitted and how are they learned? Are folk terms used to fit a pattern of a folk group? What about grammar? Folk naming? Pronunciation? Ethnic speech patterns?

Consider the following. All of the types of folk speech covered in this book were collected in the St. Louis area. They developed from all the standard folk traditions and transmissions. Other regions may have the same variants of the expressions or words or naming or grammar or pronunciation. But informants from St. Louis have used the lingo as "special" to them through their folk group, family, or even as "codes" for bonding. Often the words obviously flout correct grammar; often the speech is a permanent vestige from one's youth; often the naming is recognized only by the family, but used "knowingly" when it becomes "standard"; sometimes the foreign language becomes a new word; very often nicknames persist. Always the folk speech is transmitted orally and represents the culture of the folk group.

Family Lingo

The dialogue of families, through the years, is a clear example of the function of folklore to solidify the family culture. The expressions that families use, whether in pronunciation, grammar, or vocabulary, often become standard within the nuclear family and over time become important even to the extended family. "Baby talk" or "teen talk" can become the "official" language, which remains acceptable into adulthood. Sometimes family speech is even adopted by other groups and becomes a regional dialect.

St. Louis informants use family lingo in many forms to help them keep and maintain their lore.

"Loney" is bologna and is sometimes "fried loney."

And you can put loney on a "sammich." or "sangamon."

"Roni" is the favorite pizza at Imo's.

Sometimes they sell "zippa" at Imo's, too.

Do you want "chechpup" on your fries?

How about some "catch cup" instead?

Ranch dressing for veggies is a "dip-dip."

A kitten is a "titty tat."

Everyone eats "pasketti," or goes to the St. Louis restaurant of the same name to buy it!

St. Louisans love "girl cheese" with tomato soup.

St. Louis kids get their food at "Old McDonald's."

That airplane that lands on Children's Hospital in St. Louis is a "hopperchopper."

"Hang-a-booger" is used for hamburger.

Kids watch their dads "lawn the grass."

Some St. Louis kids wear "yamas" when they go to bed.

"Butt burp" is encouraged for flatulence. And then someone replies, "Excuse you butt."

"Hanitizer" is the same as hand sanitizer.

It can be red, black, brown, or even rainbow colors, but it is always "lick-a-wish."

Children don't have a bowel movement; they go "potty," "poo-poo," or "poopy" just as their parents do!

Some kids and even their parents go "grunty."

When a person's nose runs, they need a "booger sucker," as they used as children.

"Panny-cakes" are very good with maple syrup.

Headaches require "aspereens."

Babies' hearts "tump and tump."

Women don't have a vagina; they have a "ti-ti."

Driving in the rain requires "winchell" wipers.

Sometimes fast food restaurants sell "chicken nuts."

Listen to your family "folk talk." Did you hear it when you were younger? Do you still use the word, phrase, or pronunciation? More importantly, did you pass it on to your own family? You are living lore!

Aks or Ask? Go By? Anthat?

The way a word is pronounced or is used grammatically helps to identify a lingo. Whether ethnic in origin or learned just from "living" or identified with a folk group, St. Louis informants, who say they "know better," continue in their folkways.

It snew yesterday.

He was borned in 1942.

I seen that movie last year.

Go "figer" it out.

He's a good "athalete."

We will "probly" "go by" the store tomorrow.

"Supposeably," he's coming home tomorrow.

She goes to college in "Clumbia."

"Sundy" is either a day of the week or an ice cream treat.

Goethe, a street in St. Louis, is pronounced "go-thee," not "gur-ta" like the author.

If you go "down by the gravois," you go down by the "grav-oy."

In an emergency, a St. Louisan called an "amblance."

My friend lives "acrost" the street.

One is "spost to" trick or treat on Halloween in St. Louis.

St. Louis teens can be "mischeeveous."

Some from St. Louis go on a "toar" to Europe.

A large cemetery in St. Louis is named "cavalry."

Cameras in St. Louis used to use "fillum."

Sometimes people in St. Louis "orientate" and "interpretate."

There are "miniture" golf courses.

When ill, sometimes a person needs a "perscription."

Some people get their pets "spade."

Too often we take each other for "granite."

People keep their clothes and other things in a "chester drawers."

Someone needs to use the "Heineken" maneuver on a person who is choking.

What is his "heighth"?

St. Louis handymen always use "duck" tape.

I got this book at the "libairee."

Many people in St. Louis "prespire."

"Mayonnaise" is never pronounced "mayo."

"Sose" I can see her when she comes for vacation.

The "realator" sold me the house, not the realtor.

It's never a dog-eat-dog world, but always a "doggy-dog-world."

The people in "Illinoise" have higher taxes.

Do you soak your "dodger" in a "concrete."

Beyond the lore of the family, there is folk vocabulary peculiar to the St. Louis region. Words or expressions are used regularly in conversation and become traditional speech for the area. And they are passed on in an "unlearned" learning experience.

People don't have an idea, they have a "weenie" in St. Louis.

A "dodger" is a hard biscuit but used in a phrase to accept a dinner invitation: I'll soak up my dodger in your soup any-time.

A "concrete" is a very thick malt or shake. The famous Ted Drewes Custard in St. Louis coined the term but its application has become wider.

If you are having "mustgo" for dinner you are having leftovers. Everything in the refrigerator "must go."

A dragonfly can be a snake doctor, a witch doctor, a darning needle, or a "snake feeder."

A "brown cow" is an ice cream treat made with vanilla ice cream and root beer. A "black cow" uses Coca-Cola with the ice cream. A "red cow" uses Vess cream soda and vanilla ice cream, and an "orange cow" uses Vess' Whistle soda.

"Go on with your rat killin" is used when someone is very

busy and unable to stop and talk. The visitor replies, "Go on with your rat killin' and I'll talk to you later."

When things in the house are messy and cluttered, one says, "things are all over the hurricane deck."

When there is a lack of rain in St. Louis, they are having a "drouth."

When someone uses a restaurant's bathroom without eating there he went in for a "McPee."

A person who does not take care of himself is a "slop-hannus."

When you "dine and dash" in St. Louis, you eat at a restaurant without paying the bill.

After eating a large meal, some St. Louisans say they are in a "food coma," and need to take a nap.

If your guest overindulges on the food, he can be called a "hodger."

One who craves a cigarette is having a "nicfit."

When food is left in the refrigerator and becomes moldy, it's called a "science project."

"Toasticles" are those crumbs from the toast left in the butter.

A wild party in St. Louis is known as a "rager."

A "45-minute Catholic" is a person who attends Mass irregularly and does not stay for the entire service.

Women use a "skillet" to fry food, not a frying pan.

A guy who is not attractive or appealing but dates lots of women is a "Marlon Blando."

A woman who wears a lot of jewelry is called an "ice queen."

A very wealthy person is known as a "jillionaire."

A lady who wears a lot of makeup is a "raccoon."

The melting snow that is mixed with dirt is called "snirt."

If you want fried potatoes in St. Louis, you have to ask for "pan fried" or "German fried."

Some people have "goose bumps" when they get cold and others have "chill bumps."

Do you have a "funny bone" or a "crazy bone"?

Fishermen like to use "night crawlers" or "angleworms" for bait.

If you like pastries, do you like "bear claws," "bismarcks," "sinkers," or "crullers"?

A heavy rain is a "goose-drownder" or a "toad-strangler."

Are you a "couch potato" or a "davenport potato"?

"Bingo wings" refers to the fat which hangs from a person's upper arms. The "blue-haired set," another folk term, coined the word.

When you spend too much time at the mall you can get "mallitis."

If your eyebrows are too thick, you have "eyebrellas."

Waitresses call poor tippers "chicken feeders."

A "plum smuggler" is an elderly man who wears Speedos at the beach.

After a big night of drinking, you might wake up with a "lung cookie."

A person who talks too much to the point of exhaustion has taken a "mental laxative."

A man with large, sagging breasts has "breasticles."

A "McGirl" is a good-looking clerk at a fast food restaurant.

The Catholic method of birth control is called "Vatican Roulette."

It's raining like a cow pissing on a flat rock.

"Blind fish" is the name given by Catholics to food eaten during Lent. Eating fish is a popular meal during the weeks before Easter. Fish fries are becoming a folk custom of their own. But when some get tired of eating fish so often during the season of Lent, they make pancakes or eggs or French toast and call it blind fish.

People in St. Louis ask you to sign your "John Henry" instead of the proverbial "John Hancock."

"Corn bread" is wedding cake for a St. Louis hoosier.

A person who is articulate or glib has great "wordage."

A "sookie" is a cookie drenched in milk.

If you only wear designer clothes you are a "label whore."

When a person gets into trouble through his own fault, he "stuck his fork in the toaster."

An "Amway Christian" is one who believes that wealth is a gift from God and aggressively pursues it.

A "chocolate teapot" is a person who is useless.

"Five-finger discount" is stealing from a store.

St. Louis college students have "stoplight parties." If one wears red, he/she is taken. If one wears green, he/she is available. Finally, yellow means that the person is in a complicated relationship.

A person who browses self-help bookshelves hopes to get "shelf esteem." This can refer to a person who is always quoting some psycho-babble from television.

A St. Louis person who constantly surfs the web for medical sites looking to define the "illness" is called a "cyberchondriac."

Some people are encouraged to "go primitive" or use the phone instead of trying to communicate something complicated over the computer.

A person whose hair does not move in the strongest wind has "lego hair."

Can You Say That on TV?

One of the functions of folklore is that it permits that which is not permissible. Children are generally punished for saying "bad" words. But if a child holds his tongue and says, "Polly sits in the corner," the word "sits" will be "folk" pronounced as a "bad" word. Using the folk gesture of holding his tongue and then transmitting in the oral tradition makes it permissible.

This application of folklore works with jokes, proverbs, folk beliefs, jump rope rhymes, and even autograph book verses. The "adult" in the child is using the folkways to enter another folk group. But the child never seems to leave the world of adult folk vocabulary. For example, it is not proper to use swear words in "official" settings, like work or social affairs. But the folk, using the creativity of their youth, develop a lingo that is permissible with the euphemism barely hiding the intended words. A whole folk culture has evolved from these folk expressions that are not limited to any one folk group. They cross all folk mores.

Here are some folk terms for "permissible" profanity from St. Louis informants:

Fudgesicles on a corn stick!   What the Frog!

Full of horse apples   Dog Biscuit!

Sugar Honey Iced Tea!   Horse Hockey or Horse Feathers!

Son of a pup!   Son of a Beaver!

Son of a bugger butt!   Mother Farter!

Oh, truck!   Melon Farmer!

H-E-double hockey sticks!   Judas Priest!

Shut the front door!   Martha Cotton Picker Stewart!

Cheese and Rice!   Frick-a-frack!

Are you freakin' crazy?   Go blow it out your ear!

Son of a Mother Trucker!   Oh, sheep!

Son of a Motherless Goat!   I fardled that right up!

I Don't Give a Donald Duck!

Do you recognize the intended profanity in any of the examples? Linguists call this form of folk vocabulary a "minced oath." These expressions are made from misspelling, mispronouncing, or even replacing a part of words that are socially taboo. This allows the word to be less objectionable and acceptable in social interactions. It is believed that all profanities have a form of "mincing" inherent in them that encourages different versions, which is where the folk enter with their "permissible expressions." For example, "gosh" and "darn" are popular examples of euphemisms. They are widely known and widely used and have become a form of "meta" folklore. But the creativity of the folk, inspired and mentored by their folk group, adds variants to acceptable swearing that can be regionally specific. Depending on the culture and the circumstances, permissible profanities can reflect, describe, and define folkways of a particular group. Then passing the term on through oral transmission creates a folk vocabulary.

The Lingo of Folk Groups

By definition, folk groups use a folk vocabulary or lingoes to keep them connected and preserve their identity. The members of the group know the meaning of the terms and use them to keep others out or away from that feeling of bonding. These groups could be occupational, like lawyers, nurses, doctors, accountants, or any group with an established, learned profession. The application and use of the terms allow folk members to make their lingo even more "private."

American quilters are one of the more interesting folk groups who have an identity through their work. They are not a "profession" from their historical roots in eighteenth- and nineteenth-century America. They are domestic conservators who use scraps of their clothing to make museum-worthy quilts.

Formal classes, in the art and technique of quilting, have been offered now for decades. The quilting industry is growing at phenomenal rates, primarily catalyzed by the passion of the American folk quilter. The lingo that has developed guarantees that "outsiders" need not apply. Anyone can join the sorority of quilters if they learn the jargon and use it properly.

It is interesting to note that quilters have not only developed their own folk vocabulary, but they have also used lore to cover the whole area of traditional folklore: sayings, proverbs, beliefs, superstitions, folk poetry, jump rope rhymes, autograph book verses, customs, and even folk jeers. Often using the lore from childhood experiences, they change the folk text to be a variant related to their quilting passion. The bond becomes more secure.

Here are some examples the folk vocabulary of quilters.

How many SPIs in the quilt?

A mark of excellence in quilting is "stitches per inch." The smaller and therefore the more stitches per inch are regarded as the mark of an excellent quilter.

FAT QUARTERS: This is not a large coin! Fabric is often sold in this fashion so that the quilter can purchase a smaller amount for her quilt design. The size is 18" X 22" and sometimes referred to as an FQ.

QUILTING "IN THE DITCH": Quilters do not sit in mud and quilt. This term is used for quilt stitches made along a seam line especially in applique' quilts.

STASH: This is the collection of fabric that quilters own. The stash is more important than anything, including family!

CANDY: This is a piece of fabric that is half of a fat quarter, 11" X 18".

COC: Are you doing it COC? The quilter is asked if she is using "cream on cream."

WOW: Similar to COC, White on White is WOW and usually refers to fabric.

FART: Fabric Acquisition Road Trip, the ultimate experience for a quilter!

SHARPS: All-purpose needles.

PIGS: Projects in Grocery Bags. Every quilter has many of these which will, they promise, eventually be completed!

TRAVELING: Moving the quilting needle from one point to another through the batting.

CUTTER: A quilt in such bad shape that it can only be used by cutting it up for other projects.

BUNNY EARS: Formed in two corners when stitching a triangle and square together.

BETWEEN: This is a short needle; the higher the number, the shorter the needle.

PWF: An acronym for pre-washed fabric.

WOMBAT: Waste of Money, Batting, and Time. The sound of the word says it all!

PEANUT: Not the snack, but a piece of fabric that is 11" x 18" or even 9" x 22".

FROG: what quilters do when they undo previously completed stitches . . . rip it, rip it, and rip it! Sometimes they even make it a verb: "had to frog it," "I'm frogging it."

So, you might hear the following conversation: "I got some beautiful PWF WOW and then changed to COC and even tried to fuzzycut the last piece and tried some quilting on it and ended up frogging it. My sharps didn't work; it was even hard to ease and square. And you should have seen the bunny ears? Oh, and I even tried doing it in the ditch!" (See Chapter 7.)

There are other folk groups who have their own vocabulary and are not occupational either. College students are an excellent example. More research is needed with the group to identify texts and their applications. But verbal folklore is a definite component.

The culture of college students in addition to the need to get a degree to "make it" in the world has connotations of fun, play (there are even books documenting the most "playful colleges" in the United States), and "letting go." The thinking here is that after four years (if parents are lucky!) the leisure of youth is over and now the "real life" begins. So college students, through fraternities, sororities, clubs, social groups, and even in academic disciplines, develop their own ritual lore that is passed on to future students.

Pick-Up Lines

Good examples of academic lore are "pick-up lines," used to confirm a date and euphemisms of vaguely taboo subjects, such as words for "butt," and expressions when a guy's fly is open. College student informants from the many universities and colleges in St. Louis have used the following examples to function as glue to their folk group. Some, of course, have "leaked" from the colleges and are used in the mainstream, which underscores the importance of the transmission of folklore.

I know a great way to burn off the calories in that pastry you just ate.

Your lips are kinda wrinkled; mind if I press them?

What do you like for breakfast?

Why don't you surprise your roommate and not go home tonight?

Hi, I'm gay; think you can convert me?

Walk up to a lady simply holding a screw in your hand.

Hey, baby, do you want to come to my fortress of solitude?

It's a good thing I have freeze breath because you look dangerously hot.

Excuse me, I'm from another planet. Do you want to teach me about human anatomy?

I'm an organ donor; need any?

Want to see Santa's little helper?

I know when you've been good and bad so let's just skip the small talk.

Nice wrapping but I need to inspect it.

Shouldn't you be sitting on top of the tree, Angel?

I do like milk and cookies, but I'd rather have you.

You make the Queen of Sheba look like a hobo.

Do you need prayer? I'm willing to lay my hands on you.

I didn't believe in predestination until I met you tonight.

You float my ark.

Can I take you into the Promised Land?

You had me at Shalom!

I must be hunting treasure cause I'm diggin' your chest.

Are you Google? Because you have everything I'm searching for.

I can infer that you are smart enough to go out with me

Every time I hear your voice it reverberates within my soul.

You have the propensity for taking my breath away.

Lady, you are fine. I'll bet you have more followers than Lady Gaga.

Nice set of floppies.

Isn't your email beautifulgirl@mydreams.com?

Your homepage or mine?

Hi, the voices in my head just told me to go over and talk to you.

My love burns for you like a dying phoenix.

Hey baby, you may not be the most beautiful girl here but beauty is only a light switch away.

Come back to my place and I swear if you don't like it I'll give you a full refund.

Will you help me find my lost puppy? I saw him go into the hotel over there.

Did it hurt when you fell out of heaven?

Hi, are you by any chance taking applications for boyfriend?

If I had a nickel for every girl as beautiful as you, I'd have five cents.

You're so sweet, I'm getting cavities.

Hi, I'm incredibly rich.

Excuse me. Do you have a band-aid? I skinned my knee when I fell for you.

You must be the cause of global warming.

I don't think even a firefighter could put you out.

If I were you, I'd go out with me.

Hand a girl a small bag of sugar and say, "You've dropped your name tag."

Excuse me. Can you do me a favor and stop being so adorable?

My love for you is like diarrhea: I just can't hold it in.

Did the sun come up or did you just smile at me?

I was wondering if you had a moment to spare for me to hit on you.

Is there an airport nearby or is that my heart taking off?

Do I know you? You look a lot like my next girlfriend.

Does it matter where here is if I'm there?

What's a nice girl like you doing in a dirty mind like mine?

Can you please scratch my back; my arms are too muscular to reach.

What's a nice girl like you doing in a chatroom like this?

PICK-UP LINES FOR WOMEN:

Aren't you the guy who's supposed to buy me a drink?

Kiss me if I'm wrong, but isn't your name Tom?

What else do you want for breakfast? I already have eggs.

Informants think that pick-up lines are meant to be cheesy. Some are convinced that they work. Others just like to pass them on. Did you notice that some of the lines were derivatives of popular culture? Note also the importance of the computer in the way a come-on is spoken. Even female college students use some of the lines listed and others reflect the changes in sexual orientation. But all of the lines are learned in a folk group and transmitted within the same folk.

As mentioned above, academic folklore contains folk words for many different everyday things. Everything from saying that someone or something is stupid (see Chapter 3) to defining senior citizens to connecting with professors or college classes, like Rocks for Jocks, the geology class all athletes take because it's easy. It should be noted that this slur adds a dimension to the folk group of college students' thoughts on athletes (see Chapter 3).

The J-Lo Thing?

Consider their take on names for buttocks. This "pretended obscene" form of folklore connected with permitting what is not permissible connects to functions of lore when they were children. In college, however, and free from parental oversight, the vocabulary becomes more creative and descriptive certain to be passed on.

Badonkadonk	Bumper rumper
Pooter	Back door
Pooper	Turd cutter
Big Booty Judy	Cheeks
Tuckus	Rump
Pressed ham	Tushy
Broad in the beam	Cute dumper
Caboose	The back of my front

Patootie

Whoopie cakes

Haunches

The moon

Apple

Glutes

Rumpalicious

Lovely lady lumps

Poop deck

Wazoo

Keister

Hindquarters

Aunt Bertha

The round mounds

Her Royal Rotundness

The Big Boo-Yah

Love bubble

Poop shoot

Giganto

Maxi hiney

Onion booty

Chocolate speedway

Fart valve

Fudge tunnel

The Georgia Peach

The clapper

Buffy the body

Lucy caboosey

Wide load

The muffin

Money maker

Turdlurcher

Seat warmer

Seat cushion

South end of a north-bound horse

John Madden

Some other examples of academic/collegiate folklore are expressions related to a man's fly being open when he doesn't realize it. These are perfect examples of college students, now "adults," being comfortable with the interchange that began uncomfortably in grammar school. During the maturation process in elementary school, it was embarrassing for a boy to be called out for not having zipped his zipper. The most popular expression was

Our next guest is someone who needs no introduction.

The Buick is not all the way in the garage.

"XYZ" meaning, "examine your zipper." If a young lady uttered the phrase, the embarrassment was heightened. But the young participants were experiencing a part of what "growing up" meant. They were learning interactions between the sexes but, at that point, they only had limited knowledge.

By the time they were college students, however, they "knew" all they needed to know. Having a "fly" open became grounds for acceptable teasing since everyone knew the rules. But, college students reverted to their childhood for euphemistic folk expressions. Most of the following descriptions were collected from several fraternities and sororities at St. Louis colleges and universities in the 1990s, but some are obviously of a more recent origin. College students as a folk group keep the "tradition" alive.

Paging Mr. Johnson, paging Mr. Johnson.

Elvis Junior has left the building.

You've got a security breach at Los Pantalones.

I can see the gun of Navarone.

Someone tore down the wall and your Pink Floyd is showing.

Your soldier is not so unknown now.

Quasimodo needs to go back to his tower and tend to his bell.

You've got Windows in your laptop.

You've got your fly set for Monica instead of Hillary.

You need to bring your tray table to the upright and locked position.

Mini Me is making a break for the escape hatch.

Clearly folk vocabulary is operating in a functional way. The expressions of youth, enjoyed as a function and lesson of childhood, are enhanced with the freedom of the adult college student, which are frank but still euphemistic expressions. The phrases have taken on references to popular culture or even current affairs. All is done without explicit terminology permitting, again, what is not permissible, but still "college clever."

Collecting all the folk vocabulary related to St. Louis requires extensive work in folk grammar, pronunciation, and syntax. Add to these linguistic classifications the large number of folk groups who have their own lingo and use it for many purposes, but especially to keep their group intact and bound together. (See Chapter 7.) But the effort to collect and document the entire lingo is important to reflect trends, popular culture, thought and mobility patterns, and the dynamics of change. Essentially, what is the identity reflected in the lore? What issues are important to the folk? Does validation of a group come from their lore? Is there a true education in the "unlearned" learning process? And some basic questions related to each folk text, like: Do pick-up lines really work?

But these "words" are not just words or an identifiable lingo. They can lead to complex folk traditions in legends, superstitions, or even proverbs. The term "hoosier" is a good example of folk variation.

Indiana is known as the "Hoosier State." It is term of endearment, welcomed by everyone, publicized and proudly spoken. And the term is stamped on any and all things. In St. Louis, however, the term "hoosier" has taken on a different meaning. There are entire folk groups who try to define a "hoosier" in St. Louis. Even some popular, daily radio programs have joined in the folk play by inviting listeners to call in with their definitions. This exercise has led to a lengthy collection of folk vocabulary related to a "St. Louis Hoosier." Other regions might refer to these expressions as "redneck." Perhaps they are, but even the term "redneck" is publicly and proudly used in the mass media and transmitted as fun. There is not the strong, negative connotation that is attached to "hoosier." The theme is usually the same: illiterate (perhaps), unintelligent (perhaps), uncouth, and low class. But they are transmitted as self-effacement within the group; not so with the passing on of "hoosier." Here are some examples of lists defining a hoosier and hoosier vocabulary.

YOU MIGHT BE A HOOSIER

. . . if you use lard in bed.

. . . if you own more than three shirts with cut-off sleeves.

. . . if you have ever spray painted your girlfriend's name on an overpass.

. . . if you consider a six pack of beer and a bug zapper quality entertainment.

. . . if your lifetime goal is to own a fireworks stand.

. . . if someone asks to see your I.D. and you show them your belt buckle.

. . . if your mother does not remove the Marlboro Light from her lips before telling the state patrolman to kiss her ass.

. . . if directions to your house include "turn off the paved road."

... if your dog and your wallet are both on a chain.

... if you owe the taxidermist more than your annual income.

... if you ever lost a tooth opening a beer bottle.

... if Jack Daniels makes your list of most admired people.

... if your wife's hairdo has ever been ruined by a ceiling fan.

... if you see no need to stop at a rest stop because there's an empty milk jug in the car.

... if you have a rag for a gas cap.

... if you have a Hefty bag on the passenger side of the window of your car.

... if you have ever barbecued Spam on the grill.

... if you've ever had to scratch your sister's name out of the message "For a good time call..."

... if your brother-in-law is also your uncle.

... if Redman chewing tobacco sends you a Christmas card.

... if you bought a VCR because wrestling comes on while you're at work.

... if your dad walks you to school because you are in the same grade.

... if you view the next family reunion as a chance to meet girls.

... if your wife has a beer belly and you find it attractive.

... if you prominently display a gift you bought at Graceland.

... if your house doesn't have curtains, but your truck does.

. . . if your front porch collapses and kills more than three dogs.

. . . if you can call the boss "dude."

. . . if you think Volvo is a part of a woman's anatomy.

. . . if you consider your license plate personalized because your father made it.

. . . if you have ever been fired from a construction job because of your appearance.

. . . if you need one more hole punched in your card to get a freebie at the House of Tattoos.

Uncivilized? Not the norm? All have the same connotation, spoken as "blonde jokes" and the familiar "Polack joke," which were transmitted in another time. The informants who offer these definitions do so with the same folklore functions: bonding, superior/inferior positions, validation of a lifestyle, and integration. Ask for more information and the folk will even tell you where the "hoosiers" in St. Louis live!

Apparently, also, the "hoosier" has his own specific vocabulary. Taken on its own merits, the language is positive as a bonding for the defined "hoosier" and understood by them only. But it is meta-folklore passed on by the same folk who define them. Here are some examples of the way in which the St. Louis folk, in a clear superior/inferior stance, suggest lingo for hoosiers.

HOOSIER'S DICTIONARY OF MEDICAL TERMS

ARTERY: The study of paintings

BACTERIA: Back door to cafeteria

BARIUM: What doctors do when patients die

BENIGN:	What you be after you be eight
CESAREAN SECTION:	A neighborhood in Rome
CAT SCAN:	Searching for Kitty
CAUTERIZE:	Made eye contact with her
COLIC:	A sheep dog
D&C:	Where Washington is
DILATE:	To live long
ENEMA:	Not a friend
FESTER:	Quicker than someone else
FIBULA:	A small lie
GENITAL:	Non-Jewish person
GI SERIES:	World Series of military baseball
HANGNAIL:	What you hang your coat on
IMPOTENT:	Distinguished, well known
LABOR PAIN:	Getting hurt at work
MEDICAL STAFF:	A doctor's cane
MORBID:	A higher offer than I bid
NITRATES:	Cheaper than day rates
NODE:	I knew it
OUTPATIENT:	A person who has fainted
PAP SMEAR:	A fatherhood test
PELVIS:	Second cousin to Elvis
POST-OPERATIVE:	A letter carrier
RECOVERY ROOM:	A place to do upholstery
RECTUM:	Damn near killed him
SECRETION:	Hiding something

SEIZURE:	Roman emperor
TABLET:	A small table
TERMINAL ILLNESS:	Getting sick at the airport
TUMOR:	More than one
URINE:	Opposite of you're out
VARICOSE:	Near by

Note the folk grammar and the folk pronunciations used in the list. "Hoosiers," apparently, even have their own folk dialect in St. Louis. To some they have become a staple in St. Louis folklore and have their own jokes, folk foods, and folk art. In fact, St. Louis folk tell us you will never hear a hoosier say the following statements:

- Honey, I think we should sell the pickup and buy a family sedan.
- I'll take Shakespeare for 1000, Alex.
- We don't keep firearms in this house.
- Has anybody seen the sideburns trimmer?
- You can't feed that to the dog!
- No kids in back of the pickup; it's just not safe.
- We're vegetarians.
- Too many deer heads detract from the decor.
- Just give me the small bag of pork rinds.
- The tires on that truck are too big.
- Does the salad bar have bean sprouts?
- My fiancee, Bobbie Sue, is registered at Tiffany's.
- I just couldn't find a thing at Wal-Mart today.

- Checkmate.

- I've got it all on the C drive.

- I thought Graceland was tacky.

How strong is the "hoosier" folklore? St. Louisans even play "Hoosier Bingo." They have taken a popular folk game, put it on paper, and passed it around to the members of their folk group. Note that each section on the card describes a "hoosier," adding a new text of a "folk costume" in some of them.

The folk culture in St. Louis has spoken. One folk group is clearly defined and the oral traditions continue. Undoubtedly, another culture will become the subject of folk bantering. Patterns of folkways change, but the central theme never changes. It is not a big jump to replace "hoosier" with another term. It can just be "passed on."

Together, all these examples of lingo and folk speech can help to define a region. There are obvious variants in the examples and, certainly, in regional approaches. Can the "dominant" folk group culture set the standard for speech? How influential is the lingo if they do? What do the lingo and speech patterns reflect about the culture? What latent folk group will change the rules?

Perhaps all the collecting of folk vocabulary, lingo, grammar, pronunciation, naming, syntax, and euphemisms, among others, is related to the difficulty in the American language itself. Working with ethnic groups who have immigrated to the St. Louis area during the past several years underscored the confusion in our language. The following has been passed around to several different ESL groups as a joking example of American English. It was meant to make them less frustrated in their attempt to learn to speak St. Louisan. It is not folklore in the traditional sense, but it serves as an instruction, perhaps even a warning, that language, even folk language, has meaning and must be used carefully.

Hoosier Bingo

B	I	N	G	O
Obese lady wearing t-shirt: "Not that into you"	Lady dragging her child on a leash	Man in overalls and no shirt	Woman wearing t-shirt: "I like it against the wall"	Lady breast-feeding baby while he sits in cart
Obese woman with skirt or shorts and a wedgie	Plumber's crack on obese man	Man wearing a house-arrest alarm on ankle	Woman shopping in pajamas	Senior citizen wearing a hat shaped like a large hot dog
Man wearing t-shirt: "Fart now loading"	Baby sleeping in cart with all purchases piled over him	Woman wearing garbage bag skirt	Entire family wearing NASCAR apparel	Woman wearing fishnet stocking and shorts
White girl with 3+ multi-racial kids	Man without teeth	Woman in orange juice–can hair curlers	Unattended child crying wearing only a diaper	Man sleeping on cot in sporting goods store
A man wearing pumps	Man wearing a Rebel flag t-shirt	Woman with skunk hair—half black, half white	Pregnant lady in short shorts, halter top, and tramp stamp tattoo	Dirty diaper in shopping cart

RULES

- Spot five hoosiers—vertically, horizontally, or diagonally—at any Wal-Mart, K-Mart, Big Lots, or flea market in St. Louis
- Redeem for genuine mullet, toupee, or muskrat wig at service counter
- Cover-all on Saturdays
- Those wearing blue or red camoflauge clothes are not eligible to play
- Hoosier DNA is grounds for disqualification

The Reasons American English Is Hard to Learn:

The bandage was wound around the wound.

The farm was used to produce produce.

The dump was so full it had to refuse more refuse.

We must polish the Polish furniture.

He could lead if he could get the lead out.

The soldier decided to desert his dessert in the desert.

I did not object to the object.

After a number of injections, my jaw got number.

I had to subject the subject to a number of tests.

The wind was too strong to wind the sail.

When shot at, the dove dove into the bushes.

Since there is no time like the present, she thought it was time to present the present.

The insurance was invalid for the invalid.

To help with the planting, the farmer taught his sow to sow.

How can I intimate this to my most intimate friend?

When I saw a tear in the painting, I shed a tear.

Why are wise men and wise guys opposite?

Why do noses run and feet smell?

Note the folk expressions in the proper English usage. Does the lingo intrude to explain the proper word? Be careful out there!

CHAPTER 2

Urban Belief Tales

Perhaps the most popular form of folklore recognized by most people are urban belief tales. These are stories, told as true, about unusual happenings in a specific region. The subject matter usually revolves around a caution, or warning about some horrible criminals or a scam or a place to be avoided. There are always foreign objects found in some fast food restaurant servings. Someone is always lurking at a large discount store hoping to kidnap an unwatched child. The hooked man on lovers' lane never seems to go away. And many of the products made in foreign countries are filled with rodents or poisonous insects.

The particulars of the urban belief tales seem plausible: place, time, people involved, and the action committed. And the person telling the tale swears by its authenticity as "they know" a friend who experienced the crime. Or there is a friend of a friend (FOAF in folklore terms) who was involved. The tales pick up more details as they are passed around, usually concluding with a moral. Senior citizens are warned to be careful; teens are cautioned to watch carefully; kids are guarded with extra concern. But in almost every tale studied, folklorists cannot verify the actual happening. Digging to the very core of a tale, almost every time, leads to a dead end. Now, in some cases there are tales which were occurrences in a region and reported as a crime. But the urban belief was exaggerated to a point where the objects of the tale were varied.

The news media has picked up on many of these stories and reported them as actually happening. Even advice columnists write about them, ending with their cloying concern and warning. All this helps the tale to be passed on to many different folk groups to be applied as education for the listener or verification of a belief about the culture.

Technology, too, with its ever-changing configurations, seems to create its own tales. There are countless "true" stories of an uninformed person putting a cat or puppy in a microwave to dry them off. The use of the microwave (technology!) is foreign to some people. And the tales develop legs!

The Beehive Hairdo

One of the earliest forms of the urban belief tale collected involves the way in which high school coeds fixed their hair in the latest fashion. During the fifties and even sixties, the beehive hairdo—an upswept formed cone of hair that resembled a beehive—was the rage and required to be "in." Following the beehive and even simultaneous with it was the large teased hair which resembled cotton candy and was preserved with hair spray.

At several girls' high schools in St. Louis, stories about these girls and their hair styles developed into good gossip and a warning. The following was collected from students at Laboure and St. Mark's high schools in St. Louis. Both were all female at one time and both are now closed. Former students, who are active alumnae, recall these stories easily with great detail. Here is one example:

Judy came to school about two weeks ago with her hair in a beehive. It was unusually high and firm but it didn't seem to bother her. It was going on the third week of her hair style and there seemed to be no attempt to change it. Everybody was talking about how dirty her hair must be. Even the same ribbon was on the hair. All of a sudden in study hall, she screamed and fell over. The school nurse came in and they rushed Judy to the hospital. Blood was running down her neck into her back. The doctors undid her hair and guess what they found?: a nest of black widow spiders. They had bitten her and she died that very day. Judy's mother said she tried to make her daughter change her hair, but she wouldn't listen.

In some of the stories there are harmless bugs in the hair, or even ants. But the more dramatic black widow is the most popular form of the story. The moral of the story, of course, is the foolishness of vanity, keeping up with the styles to the point of discomfort, some need for a concept of positive self-esteem, or listening to parents when they complain of your foolish actions.

The moral is not really so different from similar urban tales today. The beehive is no longer a popular hair style, but other teenage fashion styles can produce similar results if carried to the extreme. Parents are always issuing cautions. The ladies today, who remember the stories very well, including the names of the girls who wore their hair in the style, now laugh at the details of the story. No one remembers the outcome the story presents, however. But they can identify with the results of fashion in our culture.

The Tanning Bed

One of the more recent urban tales which exists in many variations has to do with the tanning bed. The basic story line is that a young lady wants to present herself well for a class reunion (or wedding or family reunion or for a first date) so she goes to a tanning bed to get rid of her pale skin. Every other day she lies in the bed for a period of two weeks. Soon her family starts to smell something in the house as if it were burnt or burning. It seems to surround the young lady. She goes to the doctor who tells her that she is burning from the inside out and soon she will die.

That is the basic story which has all kinds of interesting details attached to it when told. And it is always told as true by an FOAF or a newspaper or TV report. The person is usually a young lady who "needs" to be tan for appearance. But she is never warned or told about the dangers of the heating danger of the tanning bed. The story always ends in death. (Sometimes the burning smell is so strong that the fire department is called to the house!)

The reflection: the medical reports on the dangers of the sun; the rise in melanoma cases; the mysterious technology inherent in the bed itself; the need in the culture to "appear" perfect; a warning to young ladies. So the tale reflects the current topics better than the actual reports could. Storytelling is more forceful than parental warnings, perhaps. Does the tale have believable parts? Yes. Did it ever happen the way it is spoken? Probably not. Did it ever happen? No record extant. Some informants were actually attendants at tanning bed places. They laughed at the story and said it was not true, but they continue to pass it on!

The St. Louis area is not without its own urban tales. They are variants of other regional tales but they have their own credibility because they "actually" happened in St. Louis.

The Choking Doberman in St. Louis Hills

A middle-aged lady, who lives in St. Louis Hills by herself, comes home from work to find her dog, a Doberman Pinscher, choking. She rushes him to the veterinarian where the doctor extracts two fingers from the dog's throat. The doctor cautions the lady not to return home but to call the police for an escort. She makes the call. When they arrive at the home, the police find an African-American cowering in the corner of the lady's closet. His two middle fingers on his right hand are missing. Obviously, he was trying to rob the house and was surprised by the Doberman. Fortunately, the lady did not return where she would have been in more danger. The man was arrested.

Now for the commonalities in the St. Louis version: the person involved is always a lady; the pet is always a Doberman

Pinscher; there are always two fingers in the dog's mouth; they are always the two middle fingers on the right hand; the veterinarian is always the hero; and the tale is always told as true.

St. Louis Hills is an affluent neighborhood in the city of St. Louis. Beautiful well-kept homes, tree-lined streets, recreation areas, a large park for all kinds of activities, churches, schools . . . all upscale and well-tended. The area is not considered "mixed" as most of the residents are white. Crime is minimal. Everyone watches out for each other. It is the kind of neighborhood where people on TV would say to a reporter: "Nothing like this ever happens in this neighborhood. I would expect it in other places, but not here."

So the moral? The fingers are from an African-American. Is there fear of integration? More crime? Stereotype? Why was he in my neighborhood? Crime never stops? Maybe all are correct and reflective; the tale accepts any of the conclusions.

But did the incident really happen? There is no reliable evidence. But the same tale was collected in Affton, a suburb of St. Louis, in 1980, where the fingers belonged to a Bosnian! Having left Bosnia in the former Yugoslavia because of the atrocities and warfare, Bosnians by the thousands came to St. Louis. Their number living in St. Louis is the largest outside of Bosnia itself. Of course, when they came to St. Louis, they had to be assimilated; it was not easy. They were described in so many different ways, most people did not know what to expect. In many ways, the talk about the Bosnians echoed the conversations about immigration throughout American history. The catch phrase which became a saying was: Same skin, different religion.

Eventually the Bosnians began to move out of the city proper and into the suburbs. Affton, with its affordable housing and proximity to their center, was an attraction for the Bosnian refugees. But the long-time residents of Affton did not know how to react to these new neighbors. One result: an urban tale about a choking Doberman with Bosnian fingers in his throat!

Inherent in the tale, of course, is a warning for those who deal or have to deal with the newcomers. Be careful! The assimilation has been very comfortable and cordial. Acceptance has been the rule. So why the story? Because the folk are involved!

Believe it or not, the choking Doberman story was collected in 2009 in an area known as Valley Park, also an area surrounding St. Louis. In this version, however, the dog was choking on the fingers of a Mexican. He, too, was found cowering in a lady's closet. Why the Mexican? No one knows for sure, but the government of Valley Park was considering some laws to affect illegal Mexicans who might try to work or live in the area. In fact, their deliberations made national news at the same time as the country was arguing over the issue of illegal immigration.

One more: in Imperial, Missouri, a town about 20 miles south of St. Louis, the choking Doberman story was told, also. It was collected in 2010. This time the man in the closet was a Muslim! The connection is clear and reflects the fear of America! But did it happen? NO.

So you get the picture. Urban belief tales come in variations with commonalities, but their message can be told with different morals or fears taken from the topic of the day.

Vanishing Hitchhiker at Calvary Cemetery

A very popular urban tale from St. Louis is a version of the *Ghostly or Vanishing Hitchhiker*.

During the months of April and May, on the street between Calvary and Bellefontaine Cemeteries, in North St. Louis, around midnight, a young lady is often seen walking on the side of the road. She is dressed in what appears to be a prom dress. You stop and ask her if she needs a ride. She agrees and tells you that she lives only a mile away. When you get to her house, you open the door of the car and she disappears. Even though it's very late, you go to the door and a man answers. You tell him the story and he knows the details immediately. He tells you that it was his daughter who died in an accident on her way home from the prom with her date. It was ten years ago.

This tale has made the rounds in St. Louis in the typical oral tradition. It's always in the spring of the year during prom season. It's always a girl hitchhiker and a man answers the door. The variations come in the years the girl has been dead. Some collected stories go as high as fifty years ago. The urban tale also "happened" on Lindbergh Boulevard on "dead man's curve" near Page. Another young lady was seen walking late at night on Big Bend in Webster Groves, on Gravois in front of Sts. Peter and Paul Cemetery and on Watson Road in front of Resurrection Cemetery. The results are always the same in each tale.

The message: driving and drinking? Dangers of prom night? Fear for daughters? They are all there. Again the moral is more dramatic in the telling of the story than in parental warning.

The Graveyard Bet

This tale relates to several cemeteries in the St. Louis area. It happened in many of them!

A young male teen and his date were out driving. The discussion turned to a story about a man in Bellefontaine Cemetery who was not really dead and was trying to claw his way out of his gravesite. His date was terrified at the story which she had also heard. The young teen suggested that they go to Chain of Rocks Park before he took her home. She was hesitant so he convinced her with the teenager, macho wager: he would go into the cemetery with a wooden stake, find the gravesite, stick it into the ground next to the tombstone and return to the car. When he was successful in doing the deed, she would agree to go parking with him. The girl, admiring his teenage bravado, agreed. Two hours passed. She was in the car alone and frightened. She stopped a passing police car and told the cops the story. They went into the cemetery and found the young man lying dead on the gravesite with the stake through his pants leg. Apparently he died from fright.

The moral of the tale is obvious as a cautionary story. The themes revolve around hormonal male teens, the dating ritual, and ghost stories. Each of the topics relates to supernatural legends also, but this urban tale is told as true and factual. The same thing, coincidentally, happened in Calvary Cemetery which is next to Bellefontaine. And there are other variations. Did it happen? Probably not, but the lesson from it is a longstanding caution.

The Union Station Cookie Caper

When Union Station was renovated into a destination venue, many well-known stores set up shop in the station. Mrs. Fields' Cookies was one of them. It is gone now, but the urban belief tale about it is still circulating.

A St. Louis woman's favorite dessert, even obsession, was the chocolate chip cookie from the Mrs. Fields' store. She loved them especially when they came right out of the oven. But she could not always be at the store when this happened so she decided to take a chance and call the store and ask if they would give her the recipe. The clerk told her that it would cost four-fifty and they would send it to her. The caller used her credit card and when she got the bill she saw that the cost was $450! She felt duped and angrily decided to send the recipe to every person she knew. She wanted revenge.

So many people received the recipe for the cookie and each one, with delight, was certain that it was the "secret" one from Mrs. Fields. They even had names of people who collected the recipe and "pulled one over on the corporation." The Fields' organization was forced to post notices in their stores that they never give the recipe out to anyone at any cost! The urban legend, in later folk terminology, went "viral."

This tale is still circulating even to the point where people have gone up to other Mrs. Fields' stores in the St. Louis area and have told the clerk that they make the cookie at home and don't need to buy one! Here the reflection, I think, is the little guy triumphing over the big corporation. Grass roots victories don't happen often. This tale proves it does! Did it happen? No. Do the folk care? No . . . they still pass it on.

Grandma's Groceries

An urban belief tale has been collected at St. Louis grocery stores area about a scamming Grandma. Examples came from customers and employees who worked at the National Food Stores before they were closed. They also were collected from Tom Boy and A&P stores. Even though these stores are almost all gone from the St. Louis area, the story continues to be told as a remembrance. Employees of other grocery stores, like Schnucks and Dierbergs mention how the story was once told to them. As a checker in the store they assume they were told the story by friends as a cautionary tale. But more pertinently, the long life of this urban legend certainly has some comments to make about senior citizens.

A man in his twenties was walking around a supermarket shopping for his groceries. He noticed that wherever he went a little-old-frail-looking grandma type was following him. She smiled frequently and he thought nothing of it. When he got to the checkout line the lady was directly in front of him. She confronts him with an apology: "Forgive me for staring at you. You look exactly like my son who died a month ago." As her groceries are being packed, she asks him, "Would you mind saying 'Good-bye, Mom,' as I leave?" She felt it would make her feel so much better. The young man agrees to do it.

As she leaves with all her groceries, she hears, "Goodbye, Mom." There is a tear in her eye and the same reaction from the young man who feels very good for doing the right thing. He is so caught up in the moment that he doesn't pay any attention to the cashier until she tells him that his bill is "$128.00." He shockingly complains when the cashier tells him that his "mother" said that "my son will pay for my groceries."

Of course, there are variants of the story in the amount of the groceries which each customer had or how the woman milks the whole scene with a hug or a cheek kiss. The young man usually has only a couple of items in his basket, which makes it all the more dramatic. This happened, don't forget, in several different grocery chains and was passed around at other chains.

The meaning: senior citizens can be devious, crafty, and down-right nasty? Often senior citizens can be victims of scams, but they can also perpetrate them? Seniors are living from check to check and something must be done to help them? Isn't it sad that in our society our neediest can't be helped? All have merit. Interestingly, one version collected had the lady's son killed in Vietnam which would add more drama and even romanticism to the urban tale. Did it happen? Facts are plausible but where is gullibility?

The Snake in the Carpet

A persistent theme in many urban belief tales is the foreign "thing" which is found in a product purchased from a major retailer or restaurant. Often, the thing is real. The snake found in a rolled area rug is a good example of this category of urban belief tales. This is an example:

A St. Louis couple went to a large discount store (variously Venture, Arlan's, K-Mart, Wal-Mart, or others) to buy a large area rug for their family room. They found the exact rug they were looking for and excitedly brought it home. As they were unrolling it onto their floor, the husband screamed and fell over. The wife did not know what was happening until she saw a snake crawling across the floor and under the sofa. She tried to rouse her husband, but could not. So she called 911. They arrived, captured the snake, which was poisonous, and rushed the unconscious husband to the hospital. But he died later from the bite of a venomous snake.

In some versions of the story, the husband dies. In others he is in a coma, but lives. Sometimes, also, the "creatures" crawling out of the rug are poisonous spiders, scorpions, or rats. In any case the common perpetrator is a dangerous critter. And the dangerous critter comes from a foreign country! The rugs are always made in China, Indonesia, India, Jamaica or some other exotic place. Only big discount stores carry these rugs, apparently, because one of them is always the vendor. Note: the tale is longstanding as it was collected from stores which closed in the St. Louis area long ago.

The reflection of this tale is, no doubt, obvious: don't buy foreign products; or don't shop at the big discount stores; support American manufacturing and production; don't visit such exotic places for a vacation.

The current political climate is fueling more of these "foreign" objects stories. Snakes are appearing in plants and even in tires. Black widow spiders and more scorpions are found in pillows. Parts of rodents are discovered in food products or in bagged clothing. They all belong to the cautionary tale type of belief tale. Did they happen? Probably in some places, but not nearly as prevalent as the hundreds of stories would suggest.

Smell the Perfume

One of the most recent urban belief tales is another cautionary version told to "remind your daughters, and women everywhere" that "these people are out there." The warning is usually shouted and followed with "actual" documentation of the name of the women who were confronted, where it was that the deed happened, and how the police responded. Here is one version of the story.

I was on the parking lot of Big Lots (or Wal-Mart, K-Mart, Schnucks, etc.) when I was approached by two men and a lady who were near my car. They were casually, but neatly dressed, and appeared to be selling something. They asked me what kind of perfume I wear. I asked them why they wanted to know. They told me they were selling designer perfume at very low prices. And they asked if I would be interested? I told him that I was not interested and one of the men man handed me three cards to smell just as they do in the department stores. I thanked him and told him I did not want any and I got into my car and went home.

Two days later I received an email sent to dozens of people with the warning to beware of these three people and their scam. I was cautioned to tell all the women I knew about the ruse since it was happening all over St. Louis in many locations. What is actually on the cards is ether! When a person smells it, they immediately faint and their belongings are stolen. Other more horrible things are certainly possible. When I told several of my friends what happened and to be careful, one told me that her friend had the same thing happen to her at a filling station in St. Louis!

This tale was collected from an informant personally as an FOAF "actual" tale. And I have received it four times in an email for me to warn the women in my life. It is another example of trying to attract women with things they want, like expensive perfume at a cheap price which appeals to their budget concerns. Women are again the victims as if to say they are clueless to a scam. The details match usual approaches to buying perfume at a reputable store so the ruse has some plausible details. But did it happen on all these parking lots in St. Louis? In the middle of the day when no one else is around? Probably not, but it does reflect the need to be aware in the face of media reports on the growing crime rates. New ways to rob people are always being invented; one can't be too careful anywhere with anyone. This seems to be the message. It's the same theme as in other urban belief tales with a different circumstance and different details, but with the same possible result.

Zombies

A discussion on urban belief tales in the St. Louis area would not be complete without at least a mention of tales about zombies. Technically, by definition in the science of folklore, tales about zombies are labeled as supernatural legends. The subject matter involves a creature who is "undead" as the researchers like to say. The thing is not "really alive and not really dead," but has that corpse-like quality of a third state of being. The original term usually referred to a corpse that was brought to life by some mysterious incantation. Sometimes witches or warlocks are involved and other times a psychic or a person schooled in the paranormal.

In the past several years, with the popularity of vampire movies, books, and television dramas, zombies have intruded and found a place for their story. The fascination with horror is very appealing to American audiences. St. Louis has an interesting part in this revival.

For decades, there have been tales about "zombie roads" in the St. Louis area. The theme centered on a story about a person who had died tragically on the road or street or highway where the visions are said to appear. Sometimes the zombie is a young man who had fallen off a cliff and was never found, but he appears to those brave or foolish enough to walk down the road. Other times it is a young lady who was abducted from the area and found dead on a "road." She, too, returns to get revenge for those who might be using "her road" for recreation or travel. Other stories involve suicides, mentally disturbed people who escaped from institutions, and even young lovers who stopped on the road for parking and were never heard from again.

The stories from the St. Louis area are strikingly similar to the Ghostly Hitchhiker except that the hitchhiker can usually be identified as someone who died on the road so many years ago. And the parent notifies the person seeking the information. A name is associated with the legend. Zombie Road legends exist for horror. Their details are meant to scare someone and sometimes deliver a caution to the listener.

But another dimension to Zombie Road legends is that interested and brave souls enjoy going to the places where the zombie is supposed to have appeared hoping to meet and even talk to the "undead" person. Some informants even report on organizing "parties" at these haunted places.

Perhaps the most famous story about zombie roads relates to the area near Six Flags in Southwest St. Louis County. Several roads are listed as places where zombies "live." In fact, informants report that Laurel Hill Road off Highway 109 in Wildwood (a suburb of St. Louis) is the "official" Zombie Road. Others have said that Poag Road near Edwardsville, Illinois is also filled with zombies. And many of the roads about the Meramec River, also in Southwest St. Louis are said to be zombie roads. The heights around the old Chain of Rocks Amusement Park in North St. Louis are sometimes inhabited by zombies. Apparently someone fell off the cliffs there and was never found . . . not to mention the many couples (as the stories go) who were killed while parking.

Castlewood Park, part of the extensive system of parks of St.

Louis County, is inhabited by zombies also, as is Babler State Park and Rockwoods Reservation. Also, one has to be careful at night in Valley Park. If you are driving on the Great River Road at night, zombies are said to appear in front of the Piasa Bird which is carved on the cliff near the entrance of the road near Alton, Illinois.

Again, these tales have been circulating in St. Louis for more than fifty years. But in the last ten years, spurred by popular culture, they have a new life. These stock folklore figures, who live on human brains and human flesh, are currently among the St. Louis region's most popular folk tales. Zombies are in vogue! Be careful passing on the tales!

The Dog Food Diet

A final example of a current urban belief tale is slightly different in style. There is a joke formula in the telling but a warning is used. Nevertheless it is told as believable and there are many examples among the folk asserting its validity.

Yesterday I went to Schnucks (or Dierbergs) to get a bag of dog food for my pet, Lucky. As I was standing in line waiting to check out, the lady behind me asked if I had a dog. I wanted to call her Ms. Obvious, but I thought it was a great chance to play with her. I told her I did not have a dog but I wanted to try the new dog food diet for a second time. I knew that I probably should not try it again as I ended up in the hospital the first time I tried it. I had lost sixty pounds but I was in intensive care with tubes stuck everywhere. But I thought I had not followed the diet correctly so I wanted to try again.

The idea is to put dog food pellets in your pockets and munch on them throughout the day whenever you feel hungry. They are full of nutrients so they should not harm me. The woman was very interested and even seemed shocked. She wanted to know if the dog food poisoned me. (By the way, by this time the whole line was listening to my story). I told her that the dog food did not poison me but I stepped off a curb to sniff the ass of a poodle and was hit by a car. The people behind her were laughing so loud and long they disrupted the whole store. Schnucks won't let me shop there again.

I'm retired so I have the time to think and do crazy things. Be careful of retired people.

This is a reverse scam pulled by retired people on those who are not. Again, there are more and more baby boomers retiring and their class will continue to grow in unprecedented numbers. The media has reported about their growth with many different approaches. Medicare and Medicaid is a constant in the news. Retirement "villages" are a way of life.

Also, the story, perhaps, is a takeoff on stories that seniors have a tough time making ends meet. Media accounts have told of senior citizens who are reduced to eating dog or cat food to survive. Here, then is an "actual urban belief tale" told with a more positive approach. Diets are constantly in the news. So combine their telling with stories about dog food being a staple for some elderly people. It's a clever tact and reflects the culture in more than one way.

Seniors want investment in the culture. But they also have felt that they have "paid their dues," and seen it all. Now it's time to abandon worry and stress, if possible, and test gullibility. So resort to parody. But the truth is still there.

Given the culture of fear in which we live, the speed of new information, the increasing applications for computers and other technology, and even the redefinition of societal norms, urban belief tales are certain to continue to develop. They will still be told as actual occurrences, with specific details. People will pass them on; send them on; and they will be believed. Again, there will be some small truth in the details, but it will take more reflection as there is no vacuum in folklore.

CHAPTER 3

The Dynamism of the New Folklore

The dynamic of the transmission of folklore texts has never been more apparent than the examples passed on by the computer. Some of the folklore examples are as old as sixty or seventy years, but are changed to fit the times in which they were sent. They are still anonymous and sent and received as if they are new and with each forwarding they assume a new reflection . . . the hopes, fears, beliefs, rituals, opinions, stresses of the sender. Collecting all variations of this Internet graffiti folklore is difficult because of the many versions of each example out there. At the same time, however, it is relatively easy to analyze the content and the meaning behind the message since a central theme is often present.

It appears that nothing is sacred in this new method of passing it on. Even some of the lore from the sixties, like "blonde jokes" and parodies of advice columnists contain specific topical reflections that were not spoken or even considered in earlier decades. In these, truly, there is no vacuum in folklore; it is all transmitted for a reason.

The examples that follow illustrate the variety of subject matter, the diversity of the informant, and even the current "take" on the topic. All are from the St. Louis area which, when considered as regional, can help explain a culture with more certainty.

The Stress Diet

BREAKFAST

1/2 grapefruit

1 piece whole wheat toast

8 oz. skim milk

Lunch

4 oz. lean boiled chicken breast

1 Oreo cookie

Herbal Tea

MID-AFTERNOON SNACK

Rest of the package of Oreos

1 quart of Rocky Road ice cream

1 jar hot fudge sauce

DINNER

1 loaf garlic bread

Large mushroom and pepperoni pizza

Large pitcher beer

3 Milky Ways

Entire frozen cheesecake, eaten directly from the freezer

By definition the absence of stress is death. What matters is the way in which people handle stress, or so the experts tell us. Moreover, we are constantly being told that there is more stress now than ever in a person's life. Lead by the plethora of information, the need to dominate experiences, the distressing fast pace of everything, which is increasing daily, all combined with the episodic stress when life intrudes, stress reduction techniques are constantly present. In fact, they bombard us mercilessly as they blame other overwhelming intrusions for the stress itself.

The need to diet for health or pride or personal stardom or peer pressure . . . or many other things, creates an added, often serious, stressor to those already induced. How does one reduce the level of stress?

There are techniques, of course, which are taught and advocated, but there is also humor and a "life-is-too-short" attitude. That is one message from the Stress Diet.

Importantly, the diet was collected from more than a dozen stress reduction classes in the St. Louis area, even at hospitals. Individuals who collected it then passed it on as paper lore or via the Internet. The use of humor is definitely used as a stress reliever, but this diet reflects a few American cultural tendencies. Perhaps it is no hidden message, but enjoy life it says with America's most popular foods. What a comfort an Oreo can be!

But folklore is being used in a clever new way using folk phrases and proverbs to help relieve stress. Familiar sayings, all metaphorical, are assigned points dependent on their use or overuse. The points are equivalent to calories that counter the Stress Diet.

EXERCISE CALORIE CHART

Beating around the bush	75
Jogging your memory	125
Jumping to conclusions	100
Climbing the walls	150
Swallowing your pride	50
Beating your own drum	100
Throwing your weight around	50-300
Dragging your heels	100
Pushing your luck	250
Making mountains out of molehills	500
Spinning your wheels	175
Flying off the handle	225
Hitting the nail on the head	50
Turning the other cheek	75
Wading through paperwork	300
Bending over backwards	175
Jumping on the bandwagon	200
Balancing the books	23
Beating your head against the wall	150
Running around in circles	350
Eating crow	225
Fishing for compliments	50
Tooting your own horn	25
Climbing the ladder of success	750
Pulling out the stoppers	75
Adding fuel to the fire	150
Pouring salt on the wound	50
Wrapping it up at day's end	12

Note that most calories are for those egregious activities which frustrate and anger people. All are metaphorical and synonymous with the definition of stress. Here the informants suggest that reducing stress is looking in the mirror at behavior, but interestingly it is transmitted as diet connected to stress, combining both overly emphasized in the culture.

110 Percent Really?

A byproduct of stress-related issues is a poor self image. Upon reflection people often wish they had done things differently, or had more goals, or had made different life choices. Life's stressors increase their psychological pain. Enter self-help. Bookstores, especially in the last two decades, have shelf after shelf of books which claim they can increase a person's self worth with some easily absorbed mantra or daily psychobabble exercise. The authors of these books have become popular and wealthy motivational speakers traveling the American circuit. Major corporations very often hire these speakers for annual meetings to motivate their employees with a new slogan or flavor of the month campaign. Even universities sponsor "speakers' series" where companies send their fast-track employees to sit at the feet of the latest phenom in motivational theory.

These combined forces: self-help books and motivational speaking and training have stirred the masses into "folk" thinking and even Internet graffiti. Does the method really work? The efforts to improve the company culture seem to be failing, employees say. And personal gain is not evident even under strict goal setting. Those who "have" seem to be getting more. How can I give more than 110 percent and not see positive results?

Target phrases have become part of folk vocabulary. Attitude, hard work, and even knowledge can't seem to get a person more rewards. There is proof in a mathematical formula.

What Makes 100 Percent?

Did you ever think: What does it mean to give more than 100 percent? Ever been to a meeting where you were encouraged to give over 100 percent? How about 103 percent or 118? Do these numbers mean anything? Use this formula to help answer these questions:

IF:

A B C D E F G H I J K L M N O P Q R S T U V W X Y Z are represented as

1 2 3 4 5 6 7 8 9 10 11 12 13 14 15 16 17 18 19 20 21 22 23 24 25 26

THEN:

H-A-R-D-W-O-R-K

$8+1+18+4+23+15+18+11 = 98\%$

AND

K-N-O-W-L-E-D-G-E

$11+14+15+23+12+5+4+7+5 = 96\%$

BUT

A-T-T-I-T-U-D-E

$1+20+20+9+20+21+4+5 = 100\%$

AND

B-U-L-L-S-H-I-T

$2+21+12+12+19+8+9+20 = 103\%$

AND, guess how far ass kissing will take you!!

A-S-S-K-I-S-S-I-N-G

$1+19+19+11+9+19+19+9+14+7 = 118\%$

So the conclusion with mathematical certainty is that Hard Work and Knowledge will get you close and Attitude will get you to 100 percent. It's the Bullshit and Ass Kissing that will put you over the top. Does it make sense why some people are at the top?

This exercise has become a popular game for white-collar workers throughout St. Louis. Using catch phrases or motivational lingo in the mathematical formula can lead to much more folk vocabulary. The primal scream is now part of corporate life and self-help has another meaning. Try cronyism. How about nepotism? What percentage do they give you? Still going nowhere in life? At least you have a way to relieve that stress based on mathematics!

If the formula does not give you all the stress relief you need, try pasting a bumper sticker on your car. Let the whole world know where you stand on an issue. The transmission of your philosophy will be seen or read over and over and over. There is not the anonymity of the bathroom for your scrawl. Your opinion is now clear and concise. Feel better?

Bumper Stickers

Here are some bumper stickers found on St. Louis cars:

Give me ambiguity or give me something else.

Lottery: A tax on people who are bad at math.

Hard work has a future payoff. Laziness pays off now.

If ignorance is bliss you must be orgasmic.

I don't suffer from insanity. I enjoy every minute of it.

The gene pool could use a little chlorine.

When there's a will, I want to be in it.

Always remember you're unique,
just like everyone else.

Make it idiot proof and
someone will make
a better idiot.

If you are a psychic, think HONK.

We have enough youth, how about a fountain of SMART?

OK, who put a stop payment on my reality check?

Note the frustration, even anger, in many of the statements. Popular preaching is questioned. And the folk have a new way of passing it on!

Stress has always been a part of life, and there have always been coping measures. Folkways are clever and varied. Since 9/11, however, stress has escalated, and individuals are at the mercy of authorities trying to protect them. Realistically, people know that the actions to enhance our safety are for the common good. But it is still okay to question the actions of the government.

Airport Screening: Statistics from the Department of Homeland Security, 2011

Security at airports has increased dramatically over the past decade. The trip to the airline gate can be hours, given all the procedures travelers have to undergo. Are they necessary for all of us? Do they really make a difference? The folk have their own statistics and obvious answers:

Hernias: 1,485

Transvestites: 133

Hemorrhoid Cases: 3,195

Enlarged Prostates: 7,877

Breast Implants: 86,998

Natural Blondes: 4

Terrorists Discovered: 0

Also: 235 members of Congress have no testicles

The folk have spoken and, depending on the informant, more of the American culture is revealed sarcastically. In all examples collected, however, there is never a terrorist found in the screening!

Test for Athletes

More and more recent folklore is being transmitted echoing the same theme. Simply put: the stupidity of people. But in a closer reading, the theme is more serious and meaningful to the collector and informant. The following are all examples. Note the wide range of subject matter but all with the same perspective.

All were collected at the University of Missouri–Columbia, the University of Missouri–St. Louis, Missouri State University, and Southeast Missouri State. The variations in the test description apply either to football players or basketball players. The questions vary slightly, but they are all constructed with the same simplicity.

Time Limit: One month

Standard: Must answer three or more questions correctly in order to play a sport.

1. What language is spoken in France?

2. Give a dissertation on the ancient Babylonian Empire with particular reference to architecture, literature, law, and social conditions. *OR* Give the first name of Pierre Trudeau.

3. Would you ask William Shakespeare to: a) build a bridge; b) sail the ocean; c) lead an army; or d) WRITE A PLAY

4. What religion is the Pope? a) Jewish; b) Hindu; c) Muslim; d) CATHOLIC

5. Metric conversion: How many feet is 0.0 meters?

6. What time is it when the big hand is on the 12 and the little hand in on the 5? a) bed time; b) 5:00; c) AM or PM; d) happy hour

7. How many commandments was Moses given? (Approximately)

8. What do we call people in the far north of the U.S.? a) Westerners; b) Southerners; c) foreigners; d) Northerners

9. Spell: Bush, Carter, and Clinton

10. Six kings of England have been called George, the last one being George the Sixth. Name the previous five.

11. Where does rain come from? a) Macy's; b) a 7-11; c) Canada; d) the sky; e) Prince

12. Can you explain Einstein's Theory of Relativity? a) yes; b) no; c) he wasn't my relative

13. What are coat hangers used for?

14. The Star Spangled Banner is the national anthem of what country?

15. Where is the basement in a three-story building located?

16. Which part of America produces the most oranges? a) Europe; b) Egypt; c) Florida; d) Alaska

17. Advanced math: If you have three apples, how many apples do you have?

18. What does NBC (National Broadcasting Company) stand for?

19. In what city in Missouri is the University of Missouri-Columbia located? a) St. Louis; b) Kansas City; c) New York; d) COLUMBIA

20. What holiday is celebrated on December 25? a) 4th of July; b) Easter; c) the BCS championship; d) Christmas

Welfare Statements

Following are "actual" examples of statements clients have written on welfare documents. Government workers in the St. Louis area have collected most of them and passed them around.

I cannot get sick pay. I have six children. Can you tell me why?

I am forwarding my marriage certificate and three children. one of which is a mistake as you can see.

My husband got his project cut off two weeks ago and I haven't had any relief since.

In accordance with your instructions I have given birth to twins in the enclosed envelope.

Unless I get my husband's money pretty soon. I will be forced to live an immortal life.

Please find out for certain if my husband is dead. The man I am living with can't eat or do anything until he knows.

This is my eighth child. What are you going to do about it?

I am glad to report that my husband who is missing is dead.

Excuses for Missing School

Even teachers collect "actual" lore and pass it on.

Please excuse Joey from school yesterday. He had loose vowels.

John has been absent because he had two teeth taken out of his face.

Bobby was absent yesterday because he was playing football and got hurt in his growing part.

Please excuse Mary for being absent on January 28, 29, 30, 31, 32, and 33.

My daughter was absent yesterday because she was tired. She spent the weekend with the Marines.

Please excuse Mary. She had been sick and under the doctor.

My son is under doctor's care and should not take P.E. Please execute him.

Please excuse Danny for being. It was his father's fault.

Insurance Claims

Insurance companies also have a lot of folklore to collect. These are from insurance papers explaining the reason for an accident.

My car was legally parked as it backed into the other vehicle.

The pedestrian had no idea which direction to run, so I ran over him.

I told the police I was not injured but on removing my hat I found that I had a fractured skull.

The indirect cause of this accident was a little guy in a small car with a big mouth.

I was sure the old fellow would not make it to the other side of the road when I struck him.

In my attempt to hit a fly, I drove into the telephone pole.

An invisible car came out of nowhere, struck my vehicle and vanished.

Dear Abby or Dear Ann or Dear Emily

Advice columnists are popular newspaper attractions. People, again under their distress, want to know how to handle a situation. So they go to the "experts" for advice. The questions reflect familiar societal concerns.

DEAR ABBY:

What can I do about all the sex, nudity, foul language, and violence on my DVR?

DEAR ABBY:

I am a twenty-five-year-old liberated woman who has been on the pill for two years. It's getting expensive and I think my boyfriend should share half the cost, but I don't know him well enough to discuss money with him? What should I do?

DEAR ABBY:

A couple moved in across the hall from me. One is a middle-aged gym teacher and the other is a social worker in her mid-twenties. These two women go everywhere together and I've never seen a man go into or leave their apartment? Do you think they could be Lebanese?

DEAR ABBY:

Our son writes to say he is taking Judo. Why would a boy who was raised in a good Christian home turn against his own?

DEAR ABBY:

My mother is mean and short-tempered. I think she is going through mental pause? What should I do?

DEAR ABBY:

You told some woman whose husband had lost all interest in sex to send him to a doctor. Well, Abby, my husband has lost all interest in sex and he is a doctor! Now what do I do?

DEAR ABBY:

Could you please advise me on the following problem?

I am thirty years of age and have two brothers. One of them is a Republican, a member of Congress and works in Washington, D.C. The other is serving a nine-year sentence in Joliet for repeated rapes. My two sisters are on the street and my father is living off their earnings.

My mother is pregnant by the neighbor next door and he refuses to marry her.

Recently, I met a great gal, an ex-prostitute, single and the mother of three beautiful children, one white, one black, and one Asian.

My problem is: Should I tell my girl that my brother is a Republican?

The Blonde Diary Cookbook

Blonde jokes: they never go away and now they are writing a Diary Cookbook.

MONDAY: It's fun to cook for Bob. Today, I made angel food cake. The recipe said to beat twelve eggs separately. The neighbors were nice enough to loan me the extra bowls.

WEDNESDAY: He wanted fruit salad for supper. The recipe said to serve without dressing. So I didn't dress. What a surprise for him when he brought a friend home for dinner.

THURSDAY: A good day for rice. The recipe said to wash thoroughly before steaming the rice. It seemed silly but I took a bath anyway. I can't say it improved the rice any.

FRIDAY: Today, Bob asked for salad again. I tried a new recipe. It said to prepare the ingredients and lay on a bed of lettuce before serving. Bob asked me why I was rolling around in the garden.

SATURDAY: I found an easy recipe for cookies. The recipe said to put the ingredients in a bowl and beat it. There must have been something wrong with this recipe. When I got back, everything was the same as when I left.

All of the above examples have a common folk thread: You can't fix stupid as the saying goes. Look again: The stereotype is back!

Some conclusions and reflections:

The superior/inferior tradition is alive and well in American culture.

Don't hide what you feel; put it on your car for all to see. Flout authority!

Athletes make a lot of money without the proverbial "necessary" college education and they often get jobs after their careers in fields others trained for.

Welfare is a constant argument. It's the right vs. the left in politics. It's not the American way. The recipients are unintelligent, lazy people who have no sense of responsibility.

It is no surprise that our education system is in disarray. Look at the parents!

There should be more stringent rules for driving. Look at the idiots at the wheel driving around today not even knowing how an accident occurs.

Abby, Emily, Ann, and others are not experts but think they are. Some people also think the advice columnist is smart and has all the answers. But how do they respond to the topics of the day? Is it a case of dumb and dumber? Or are the letters exposing our cultural fears or anxieties?

Own the Stereotype

For years, the folk have been collecting illogical notices from church bulletins. Either the context, the placing of the words, or the religious connotations themselves are amusing. Having been transmitted through the sacred institution of the church makes them even more relevant. The bond is immediately recognized by the congregation and the notice helps to strengthen the bond and they "get" it.

In a related example of folklore, Jews have collected and passed on similar examples from their synagogues' members. They are a clear example of the delightful, self-effacing culture of the Jewish people. They recognize, often, their own stereotypes and can joke about them in a reflective way which, again, bonds the Jewish community.

SYNAGOGUE BULLETIN BOARDS

The High Holidays have nothing to do with marijuana.

Where there's smoke, there may be salmon.

No meal is complete without leftovers.

A *shmata* is a dress that your husband's ex is wearing.

You need ten men for a *minyan*, but only four in polyester pants and white shoes for pinochle.

One mitzvah can change the world; two will just make you tired.

After the destruction of the Second temple, God created Nordstrom's.

Anything worth saying is worth repeating a thousand times.

Never take a front row seat at a bris.

Next year in Jerusalem? The year after that, how about a nice cruise?

Spring ahead, fall back, winters in Boca.

WASPs leave and never say goodbye. Jews say goodbye and never leave.

Always whisper the names of diseases.

If you have to ask the price, you can't afford it. But if you can afford it, make sure to tell everyone what you paid.

Laugh now, but one day you'll be driving a Lexus and eating dinner at 4:00 p.m. in Florida.

According to Jewish dietary law, pork and shellfish may be eaten only in Chinese restaurants.

It's clear in the new folklore that occupations and institutions with required applications are reflecting on the state of the culture. For years, or so it seems, the folk have been relatively quiet, like a silent majority, in their opinions about current events. But the new order allows responses in the form of sarcasm, or jokes to familiar stereotypes, or pompous gurus, or government dictates or rules. Who said: "There is many a truth in jest?"

Look at the final example. The folk seem to be saying that they can't take it anymore! Americans are not bright. They are dumb! No, they are stupid! So, I as a superior person have a right to define the inferior one with my own definition. A folk game has developed among St. Louis twenties and thirties clubbers. Think of all the definitions you can for somebody who is stupid. Here are some examples.

POLITICALLY CORRECT WAYS TO SAY SOMEONE IS STUPID

A few clowns short of a circus

A few fries short of a Happy Meal

An experiment in artificial stupidity

A few beers short of a six pack

Not the coldest drink in the refrigerator

Dumber than a box of hair

A few peas short of a casserole

Doesn't have all his cornflakes in one box

The wheel's spinning, but the hamster's dead

One Froot Loop short of a full bowl

One taco short of a combination plate

A few feathers short of a whole duck

All foam, no beer

The cheese slid off his cracker

Body by Fisher, brain by Mattel

Has an IQ of 2, but it takes 3 to grunt

Some people drink from the fountain of knowledge, but he just gargled

Couldn't pour water out of a boot with instructions on the heel

He fell out of the stupid tree and hit every branch on the way down

An intellect rivaled only by garden tools

As smart as bait

Chimney's clogged

Doesn't have all his dogs on one leash

Doesn't know much, but leads the league in nostril hair

Elevator doesn't go all the way to the top floor

Forgot to pay his brain bill

Sewing machine is out of thread

His antenna doesn't pick up all the channels

His belt doesn't go through all the loops

If he had another brain, it would be lonely

Missing a few buttons on his remote control

Slinky's kinked

Surfing in Nebraska

Too much yardage between the goal posts

In the pinball game of life, his flippers were a little farther apart than most

Not the sharpest knife in the drawer

No grain in the silo

Proof that evolution CAN go in reverse

Receiver is off the hook

Skylight leaks a little

Got into the gene pool while the lifeguard wasn't watching

A room-temperature IQ

A gross ignoramus is 144 times worse than an ordinary ignoramus

A photographic memory, but the lens cover is glued on

A prime candidate for natural de-selection

Bright as Alaska in December

Got a full six pack, but lacks the plastic thingy to hold them together

One-celled organisms outscore him in IQ tests

Donated his body to science . . . before he was finished with it

During evolution, his ancestors were in the control group

Fell out of the family tree

Gates are down, the lights are flashing, but the train isn't coming

Warning:
objects in mirror are
dumber than they appear

Has two brains: one is missing and the other is out looking for it

He's so dense the light bends around him

If brains were taxed, he'd get a rebate

If he were any more stupid, he'd have to be watered twice a week

If you give him a penny for his thoughts, you get change back

If you stand close enough to him, you can hear the ocean

One neuron short of a synapse

Takes him 1.5 hours to watch *60 Minutes*

As a baby, was left on the Tilt-A-Whirl a bit too long

Note that all these are "politically correct" ways to define a person. The folk are bonding in a whole new way. The message is no longer hidden and obscure. All institutions are targets. And the unaware had better become aware!

CHAPTER 4

The New Graffiti

For years, in folklore classes at major universities, students have researched the texts of graffiti written on walls. A class of buildings was never specific; the graffiti appeared everywhere. Bathrooms were the targeted areas, often decorated with prurient language, but the greater collection of graffiti folk texts on restroom walls were "primal screams."

Theories abound as to the *why* of graffiti. Common to all is the need for a person to be heard. In our ever-changing world, so much information is being disseminated, that most of it is being lost. Confusion can be the resultant state of being which can lead to stresses, withdrawal, ambiguity, lack of goals, inaction, neuroses, and even psychoses. The theory which many accept is that people don't like to be the "voice in the wilderness" and want, even need, to be heard. But most aren't listening. Walls, particularly bathrooms, are the equalizer.

In a place common to all, why not write your feelings, emotions, fears, or arguments where they can be read? Relief (in a couple of ways, I suppose) is certain! But the scrawls can be legally dangerous on walls. Enter the new graffiti and new folklore with transmission via the computer. And the space for communicating is much larger!

St. Louis groups of lawyers, a folk group always victims of jokes, enjoy devising laws not enacted by legislatures. These tongue-in-cheek declarations have the weight of the Ten Commandments in our everyday stressful existence. And they are promulgated with the same seriousness. Soon they make the rounds of folklore transmitted from the lawyers' groups to the common man who has the same experiences.

It's the Law! Don't Fight It!

LAW OF GRAVITY: Any tool, bolt, nut, screw, when dropped, will roll to the least accessible corner.

LAW OF VARIATION: If you change lines or traffic lanes, the one you were in will always move faster than the one you are not in.

LAW OF THE RESULT: When you try to prove to someone that a machine won't work, it will.

LAW OF MECHANICS: The severity of the itch is inversely proportional to the reach.

LAW OF PROBABILITY: The probability of being watched is directly proportional to the stupidity of your act.

LAW OF RANDOM NUMBERS: If you dial a wrong number, you never get a busy signal and someone always answers.

LAW OF THE BATH: When the body is fully immersed in water, the telephone or doorbell will ring.

LAW OF CLOSE ENCOUNTERS: The probability of meeting someone you know increases dramatically when you are with someone you don't want to be seen with.

LAW OF THE THEATER AND HOCKEY ARENA: At any event, the people whose seats are farthest from the aisle always arrive last. They are the ones who will leave their seats several times to go for food, beer, or the toilet and who leave early before the end of the performance or the game is over. The folks in the aisle seats, come early, never move

> **Law of Mechanical Behavior:**
> After your hands become coated with grease, your nose will begin to itch and you'll have to pee.

once, have long gangly legs or big bellies, and stay to the bitter end.

LAW OF COFFEE: As soon as you sit down to a cup of hot coffee, your boss will ask you to do something that will last until the coffee is cold.

LAW OF LOGICAL ARGUMENT: Anything is possible if you don't know what you are talking about.

LAW OF THE DOCTORS: If you don't feel well, make an appointment to go to the doctor. By the time you get there, you'll feel better.

LAW OF PHYSICAL APPEARANCE: If the clothes fit, they are ugly.

LAW OF LOCKERS: If there are only two people in a locker room, they will have adjacent lockers.

LAW OF PHYSICAL SURFACES: The chances of an open-faced jelly sandwich landing face down on a floor are directly correlated to the newness and cost of the carpet.

The lawyers, of course, speak to all of us. Context is important in lore and coming from the specific folk group of lawyers, communication and variation is inevitable. There are already many versions of Murphy's Law, but put in the vernacular of the lawyer, the folk laws appear more relevant. Interestingly, also, is the recent transmission of these "basic" laws. The political climate of the past several years is directly centered on the making and applying of laws. Folklore reflects society.

Chain Letters

Those constant, persistent, often irritating letters sent to ten or more people with the same request . . . money, recipes, prayers, plants, etc . . . all need to be sent to the people on the list. The instructions "demand" that the reader put his/her name on the bottom of the new list and within so many days the sender will receive dozens, more or less, of recipes, quarters, prayers, whatever the subject! And there is always a warning at the end: Break the chain and you will have some kind of bad luck, often from death to jail terms to losing friends! There is sometimes a testimony of the efficacy of the letter from the "friend" sender. "I can swear that this works. I have received "whatever" from people all over the country. I have new friends and new luck!"

For decades these letters were sent via the Post Office. Enter the computer! To be sure, they were constant mailings years ago, but the speed of the computer has made chain letters everyday occurrences or warnings. Neither the message nor the requests have changed. And the warning is still there, but even more dire. The ease of transmitting the request takes only one finger on a contact list. Immediate connection! Immediate results? Good luck? Bad luck? Who's to say? Follow-ups are difficult in this urban folklore.

Some people delete the chain letter immediately, but more send it on. The thinking: It can't hurt if it is for good luck, or prayers, or "working" lottery numbers. But others reply with the reactive lore of the folk. The following chain letter was sent via the computer thirteen times in the St. Louis area in the past two years. But first it was sent as an actual letter with formal letterhead from "The St. Louis Shoe Corporation," on Carondelet Boulevard in St. Louis. Many women received the letter in the mail. The message is clear.

This chain letter was started in hopes of bringing relief to other tired and discouraged women. Unlike more chain letters, this one does not cost anything. Just send a copy of this letter to your friends who are equally tired and discontented. Then bundle up your husband or boyfriend and send him to the woman whose name appears at the top of the list, and add your name to the bottom of the list. When your turn comes, you will receive 5,626 men. One of them is bound to be better than the one you already have!

YOU CAN BE LUCKY. DO NOT BREAK THIS CHAIN! One woman broke the chain and got her own son of a bitch back!!!

The main theme of this chain letter is clear. Some people are tired of getting all these letters on their computer, so they respond with an obvious, joking letter. But the warning may have some appeal for readers!!

Consider other reflections, however. The battle of the sexes is again represented. Can't get rid of your husband with a divorce? Or separation? Or murder? Someone will surely want him. One's trash is another's treasure to use a popular folk expression!

Deeper, however, is the folk belief involved. America is a nation of superstitious citizens resulting probably from our melting pot, multiculturalism, and even manifest destiny and optimism. We knock on wood and pick up pennies and eat certain foods on New Year's Day, and throw bouquets at weddings, etc. It doesn't hurt to do all these rituals; and it may help. The same principle applies to chain letters. Americans respond to them as a harmless activity, which could become a good-luck activity. The cultural climate demands the response which is diminished in less worrisome times. But they won't go away!

Everyone's an Expert

Home repair, interior decorating, new cooking methods, simplifying your life, organizing your "stuff," rules for using "color" to make something "pop," and have the "wow" factor and countless other "buzz" trends are at epidemic proportions. Entire television networks have sprung up devoted entirely to improving your "home" and "life." Make everything easier, organized, attractive, enjoyable with a few "very simple rules," is what they are telling us. And the person telling us what color to use in our living rooms has become a megastar in the folk universe. He or she is revered to epic levels. They are "goddess-like," and the folk follow.

But the folk, not surprisingly, have an opinion expressed in their terms. The "folk way" of doing things was collected from a cooking school sponsored by Dierbergs, a local grocery chain in St. Louis.

TIPS FROM MARTHA AND MY WAY

MARTHA'S WAY:

Stuff a miniature marshmallow in the bottom of a sugar cone to prevent ice cream drips.

MY WAY:

Just suck the ice cream out of the bottom of the cone, for Pete's sake.

MARTHA'S WAY:

To keep potatoes from budding, place an apple in the bag with the potatoes.

MY WAY:

Buy Hungry Jack mashed potato mix and keep it in the pantry.

MARTHA'S WAY:

When a cake recipe calls for flouring the baking pan, use a bit of the dry cake mix instead and there won't be any white mess on the outside of the cake.

MY WAY:

Go to the bakery. They'll even decorate it for you.

MARTHA'S WAY:

Wrap celery in aluminum foil when putting it in the refrigerator and it will keep for weeks.

MY WAY:

Who the hell eats celery?

MARTHA'S WAY:

If you accidentally knock over salt a dish while it's still cooking, drop in a peeled potato and it will absorb the excess salt for an instant "fix me up."

My Way:
Leftover wine?
Now that's hilarious.

Martha's Way:
Don't throw out all that leftover wine. freeze into ice cubes for future use in sauces.

If you over salt a dish while you are cooking, that's too damn bad. My motto: I made it and you will eat it and I don't care how bad it tastes.

MARTHA'S WAY:

Brush some beaten egg white over a piecrust before baking to yield a beautiful glossy finish.

MY WAY:

The Mrs. Smith frozen pie directions do not include brushing egg whites over the crust; so I don't do it.

Any folk phrase could be used here: knock off the pedestal; slay the giant; skewer the pompous pig; knock 'em down a peg or two . . . they all fit. A persistent theme in American folklore celebrates the underdog. Those who "look down their noses" with know-it-all answers are not like the common man. But the folk are powerless to change the stature of the "superstars," so as scrawls on walls, they can deflate with folk expressions and speak for many other folk groups.

Computer Customer Service: A New Language?

In folklore research, it was inevitable for the computer, so powerful in its influence, to be a part of the steady lore. The occupational folk group, computer programmers, proudly using the folk names "geeks" or "nerds," collect, very often, lore from those who are "computer challenged." The popular belief is that computers change so frequently that consumers have to buy a new one every year to keep up with the latest software. Perhaps the folk philosophy about buying the newest gadget concerns being involved in competition and keeping up with the proverbial Joneses as the cultural reflection.

St. Louis computer whizzes have collected the lore, and are amused by it. To them it is the equivalent of the dumb blonde joke that has returned to popularity recently.

Look at the following conversations between the tech expert and the computer illiterate.

TECH SUPPORT: What's on your monitor now, ma'am?

CUSTOMER: A teddy bear my boyfriend bought for me at the 7-11.

CUSTOMER: I can't get on the Internet.

TECH SUPPORT: Are you sure you are using the right password?

CUSTOMER: Yes, I'm sure. I saw my colleague do it.

TECH SUPPORT: Will you tell me the password?

CUSTOMER: Five dots.

Tech Support: Click on "my computer" icon on the left of the screen.

Customer: Your left or my left?

Customer:
I have a huge problem. A friend has placed a screen saver on my computer but every time I move the mouse, it disappears.

TECH SUPPORT: How may I help you?

CUSTOMER: I'm writing my first email.

TECH SUPPORT: OK, and what seems to be the problem?

CUSTOMER: Well, I have the letter "a" in the address but how do I get the little circle around it?

TECH SUPPORT: What kind of computer do you have?

CUSTOMER: A white one.

CUSTOMER: My keyboard is not working anymore.

TECH SUPPORT: Are you sure it's plugged into the computer?

CUSTOMER: No. I can't get behind the computer.

TECH SUPPORT: Pick up your keyboard and walk ten paces back.

CUSTOMER: OK.

TECH SUPPORT: Did the keyboard come with you?

CUSTOMER: Yes.

TECH SUPPORT: That means the keyboard is not plugged in.

TECH SUPPORT: What anti-virus program do you use?

CUSTOMER: Netscape.

TECH SUPPORT: That's not an anti-virus program.

CUSTOMER: Oh, sorry . . . Internet Explorer.

CUSTOMER: Hi, good afternoon. I can't print. Every time I try, it says, "Can't find the printer." I've even lifted the printer and placed it in front of the monitor, but the computer still says he can't find it.

TECH SUPPORT: OK, let's press the control and escape keys at the same time. That brings up a task list in the middle of the screen. Now type the letter "P" to bring up the program manager.

CUSTOMER: I don't have a P.

TECH SUPPORT: On your keyboard. Look on your keyboard.

CUSTOMER: What do you mean?

TECH SUPPORT: "P" . . . on your keyboard.

CUSTOMER: I am not going to do that!

TECH SUPPORT: Are you running your computer under Windows?

CUSTOMER: No, my desk is next to the door, but that is a good point. The man sitting next to me in his cubicle is under a window and his computer is working fine.

So, the equivalent of the dumb blonde joke, Little Audrey joke, and other jokes about ethnicities has hit the world of the computer. It's another superior/inferior argument. The expert, trying to be patient, explains the technology, but the new language is confusing to the computer illiterate. With the daily changes in computer development, certainly, more of this lore will develop and be passed on. And the techies in St. Louis and other cities can have the last laugh.

CHAPTER 5

The New Folklore of the Child

For decades collecting the folklore of kids was a major research project for scholars. Autograph book verses, jump rope rhymes, jeers, insults, song parodies, ghost stories, and folk games were the domain of kids who passed them on for many, many years. Often the same folklore verse would be collected within fifty years of its transmission. This is the traditional criterion for lore. Changes in the material collected were simply in a current slang word or phrase. But the rhythm, cadence, and application of the kids' lore were always the same.

Certainly, this children's lore is being collected today just as it was "in the day." But another variant of the lore of school children is being passed along among adults. The theme is consistent: mistakes children make in a school setting. Since no folklore is ever told in a vacuum and since every folk text, when examined, reflects the culture, these examples, funny as they are, probably relate to our educational standards. Certainly the innocence of the child, which is becoming less suspect every year, is also worthy of consideration.

Look at all the following examples. All have been collected in the St. Louis area from informants who "swear" they are "actual" student responses. The person who gathered the example knows a teacher or a friend of a teacher, or a friend of a friend (FOAF), who knows the kids who gave the answers, or who knows the principal of the school, or the administrator of the district or . . . ! Interestingly, the examples came from the St. Louis school system as well as districts around St. Louis: Affton, Arnold, Kirkwood, Mascoutah, Lemay, Wentzville, and Riverview Gardens. Curiously, the folklore was very similar for being so original and from a "certain" school. But that is the function and nature of folklore: to pass on lore reflective of the culture. No doubt other school districts in other regions have seen the same lore greatly aided by the computer. For us, these are St. Louis-generated!

Discussions with Third and Fourth Graders on Marriage

HOW DO YOU DECIDE WHOM TO MARRY?

You got to find somebody who likes the same stuff. Like, if you like sports, she should like it that you like sports, and she should keep the chips and dips coming. (age 8)

No person really decides before they grow up who they're going to marry. God decides it all way before, and you get to find out later who you're stuck with. (age 8)

WHEN IS IT OKAY TO KISS SOMEBODY?

When they're rich. (age 7)

The law says you have to be 18 so I wouldn't mess with that. (age 7)

The rule goes like this: If you kiss someone, then you should marry them and have kids with them. It's the right thing to do. (age 8)

WHAT DO YOU THINK YOUR MOM AND DAD HAVE IN COMMON?

Both don't want any more kids. (age 7)

WHAT DO MOST PEOPLE DO ON A DATE?

Dates are for having fun, and people should use them to get to know each other. Even boys have something to say if you listen long enough. (age 9)

On the first date, they just tell each other lies and that usually gets them interested enough to go for a second date. (age 8)

WHAT IS THE RIGHT AGE TO GET MARRIED?

Twenty-two is the right age because you know the person forever by then. (age 7)

IS IT BETTER TO BE SINGLE OR MARRIED?

It is better for girls to be single but not for boys. Boys need someone to clean up after them. (age 8)

How can a stranger tell if two people are married?

You might have to guess, based on whether they seem to be yelling at the same kids. (age 8)

Tell your wife that she looks pretty even if she looks like a dump truck. (age 8)

There sure would be a lot of kids to explain, wouldn't there? (age 8)

Answers to Tests by Grade School Students

FOR SNAKEBITE:
Bleed the wound and rape the victim in a blanket for shock.

FOR FRACTURES:
To see if the limb is broken, wiggle it gently back and forth.

FOR DIZZINESS:
Put the head between the knees of the nearest doctor.

TO KEEP MILK FROM GETTING SOUR: Keep it in the cow.

FOR DOG BITES:
Put the dog away for several days. If he has not recovered, then kill it.

TO PREVENT CONCEPTION: Use a condominium.

THERE ARE THREE KINDS OF BLOOD VESSELS:
arteries, vanes (sic), and caterpillars.

WHAT IS DEW?
When the sun shines down on leaves and makes them sweat.

THE MOON IS A PLANET, just like the earth, but it is deader.

WHO WAS LOUIS PASTEUR? He discovered a cure for rabbis.

MUSHROOMS always grow in damp places and so they look like umbrellas.

NAME THE FOUR SEASONS: salt, pepper, mustard, and vinegar.

BRIEFLY EXPLAIN HARD WATER: Ice

WHAT IS A FIBULA? A small lie

WHO WAS WILLIAM TELL?
He shot an arrow through an apple while standing on his son's head.

LITER: a nest of new puppies.

WHAT IS GRAVITY? It happens in the fall when apples fall off trees.

WHO WAS KARL MARX? He became one of the Marx brothers.

MAGNET: something you find crawling all over a dead cat.

MOMENTUM: what you give a person when they are going away.

RHUBARB: a vegetable that looks like celery gone bloodshot.

FOR NOSE BLEED:
put the head lower than the body until the heart stops bleeding.

WHO WERE THE ROMANS?
People who never stayed in place for a long time.

All these answers have been collected and shared by teachers, parents, administrators throughout the area. Funny, yes? Possible, yes? Misspelled words throughout are examples of a folk vocabulary that could stand alone when spoken in the oral tradition. But what do the answers say, collectively, about the state of American education?

Interviews with Second Graders:

Why God Made Moms

WHY DID GOD MAKE MOTHERS?

She's the only one who knows where the scotch tape is.
Mostly to clean the house.
To help us out of there when we were getting born.

WHAT INGREDIENTS ARE MOTHERS MADE OF?

God makes mothers out of clouds and angel hair and everything nice in the world and one dab of mean.

They had to get their start from men's bones.
Then they mostly use string, I think.

WHY DID GOD GIVE YOU YOUR MOTHER
AND NOT SOME OTHER MOM?

We're related.

God knew she likes me a lot more than other people's moms like me.

HOW DID GOD MAKE MOTHERS?

He used dirt, just like for the rest of us.

Magic plus super powers and a lot of stirring.

God made my mom just the same like he made me. He just used bigger parts.

WHAT WOULD IT TAKE TO MAKE YOUR MOM PERFECT?

On the inside she's already perfect. Outside, I think some kind of plastic surgery.

Diet. You know, her hair. I'd diet, maybe blue.

WHO'S THE BOSS AT YOUR HOUSE?

Mom doesn't want to be the boss, but she has to because dad's such a goofball.

Mom. You can tell by room inspection. She sees the stuff under the bed.

I guess mom is, but only because she has a lot more to do than dad.

WHAT KIND OF LITTLE GIRL WAS YOUR MOM?

My mom has always been my mom and none of that other stuff.

I don't know because I wasn't there, but my guess would be pretty bossy.

They say she used to be nice.

WHAT DID YOUR MOM NEED TO KNOW ABOUT YOUR DAD BEFORE SHE MARRIED HIM?

His last name.

She had to know his background. Like is he a crook? Does he get drunk on beer?

Does he make at least eight hundred dollars a year?

Did he say no to drugs and yes to chores?

WHY DID YOUR MOM MARRY YOUR DAD?

My dad makes the best spaghetti in the world. And my mom eats a lot.

She got too old to do anything else with him.

My grandma says that mom did not have her thinking cap on.

WHAT'S THE DIFFERENCE BETWEEN MOMS AND DADS?

Moms work at work and work at home and dads just go to work at work.

Moms know how to talk to teachers without scaring them.

Dads are taller and stronger, but moms have all the real power because that's who you got to ask if you want to sleep over at your friend's house.

Moms have magic. They make you feel better without medicine.

WHAT DOES YOUR MOM DO IN HER SPARE TIME?

Mothers don't do spare time.

To hear her tell it, she pays bills all day long.

IF YOU COULD CHANGE ONE THING ABOUT YOUR MOM, WHAT WOULD IT BE?

I would like her to get rid of those invisible eyes in the back of her head.

I would make my mom smarter. Then she would know that it was my sister who did it, not me.

Does the oral tradition of folklore apply to these answers about mom? Is the cleverness of the answers too pat? What about the stereotypes about mom in the answers: eyes in back of head? Diets? Working more than dad? Dad as Dagwood? Moms in control? They seem to be versions of "Momisms" which are popular folk texts among adults. Remember? Always wear clean underwear. You might be in an accident. Or never play with matches or you'll wet the bed. For generations mothers have used these moral "preachments" as warnings for their children. They have become part of the definition of the woman in American culture. Mom controls the morality of the country! The answers the kids gave in defining Mom picks up on this role as protector, teacher, moralist, and often superior. Has the lore now been picked up by kids? Out of the mouth of kids as the folk expression tells us. Beyond the laughter, it's worth reflecting on as nothing is said in a vacuum in folklore.

CHAPTER 6

Growing Older with Folklore

In interviews with senior citizens and baby boomers about the folklore of the oral tradition they transmit, consistent folk types emerge. Whether in group activities around St. Louis or in their over-50 clubs, or in retirement residences, even at regular gatherings at a coffee shop or fast-food restaurants, the enjoyment of discussing the lore of aging is paramount.

These lively discussions take on vitality that is contagious. The senior citizen folk groups are "committed" to define themselves, often through self-effacement, and are eager to educate at the same time. For example, survey after survey has shown that the folk over sixty-five and well into their eighties are using computers to remain "with it." Positively, they become part of the new method of transmitting lore while establishing their place as a specific folk group.

Also, the lore collected in the St. Louis area from the "boomer" group covers a wide range of types of lore. It's as if to say, "We are getting older, but that is an asset." The vitality and acceptance of their "deserved" age, by this folk group, is refreshing and instructional.

The following example is a direct answer to the texting of the young people's lore. Note the humor in the recognition of their own stereotypes. In this clear example, laughter can destroy any barriers and grant superiority to the senior folk group. This was collected in several senior residences in the St. Louis area during informant interviews and in several luncheon group sessions at various restaurants in St. Louis.

Texting Codes for Seniors

ATD: At the doctor's

BFF: Best friend's funeral

BYOT: Bring your own teeth

CBM: Covered by Medicare

CUATSC: See you at the Senior Center

FWBB: Friend with Beta Blockers

FWIW: Forgot where I was

FYI: Found your insulin

GGPBL: Gotta go. Pacemaker battery low

GGLKI: Gotta go. Laxative kicking in

GHA: Got heartburn again

HGBM: Had good bowel movement

IMHO: Is my hearing aid on?

LMDO: Laughing my dentures out

LOL: Living on Lipitor

LWO: Lawrence Welk's on

OMMR: On my massage recliner

OMSG: Oh, my! Sorry, gas

ROFL . . . CGU: Rolling on the floor laughing . . . can't get up

DWI:
Driving While Incontinent

BTW:
Bring the Wheelchair

TOT: Texting on toilet

TTYL: Talk to you louder

WAITT: Who am I talking to?

WTFA: Wet the furniture again

WTP: Where's the prunes?

WWNO: Walker wheels need oil

Many times these examples were passed with the declaration: we deserve our own text codes; we have earned them! But notice that the acronyms are variants of the popular ones used by the "younger" member of society. They don't BYOB, for example, they BYOT! The tongue-in-cheek humor has a message inherent. Seniors are not going anywhere and their numbers are growing, put up with us! This is a classic case of a folk group bonding and sharing common factors. More importantly, they pass on their lore, often, via the Internet, stereotypically the domain of young people. Ironically, some teenagers are using a few of these texts. A function of folklore: education!!

Perhaps in an attempt to retain some of their youth, the over-fifty crowd have developed folk games with the same intent as step ball, kick the can, hide and seek, or any other game of their youth: sharing one thing in common, validating their folk group, and more and more bonding. Actual parties in St. Louis senior groups revolve around playing a folk game, *How Do You Know You Are Getting Older?* With the help of some "loosening spirits" as they call them, the "old-timers," as they also call themselves with insincere mocking, try to think of the benefits, the rituals, or the customs of life after fifty. An added result is that memories are stirred and conversations often lead to other examples of folklore from their youth. The following were collected from several group discussions:

How to Know if You Are Getting Older

The gleam in your eyes is from the sun hitting your bifocals.

You feel like the night before and you haven't been anywhere.

Your little black book contains only names ending in M.D.

The best part of your day is over when the alarm goes off.

You stop looking forward to your next birthday.

You're 18 around the neck and 44 around the waist.

A fortune teller offers to read your face.

You burn the midnight oil at 9 p.m.

You get your exercise acting as a pallbearer for your friends who exercise.

You get winded playing chess.

Your children are beginning to look middle-aged.

You look forward to a dull evening.

You sit in a rocking chair and can't get going.

Dialing long distance wears you out.

You turn out the light to save electricity, not for romance.

Your teeth sink into a steak and stay there.

You've got too much room in the

Your back goes out more than you do.

Everything hurts and what doesn't hurt, doesn't work.

house and not enough room in the medicine cabinet.

Your knees buckle, but your belt won't.

You regret all those mistakes resisting temptation.

These "old-timers" recognize the importance of breaking down barriers using humor. They seem to know, secretly, that they are a "booming" group and their philosophy and even existence has to be dealt with. The stereotypes they use imply that they might have some concerns getting older, but they will survive!

Not only are boomers and seniors defining their place, they are looking forward to continuing in the workforce. Again, they are telling us, "We will remain a force." When they apply for a job, their age and experiences can be a benefit to the place where they are applying. The responses in a resume or application can be brutally honest. Gone are the workdays where the proper attitude was critical. It's as if to say, "I earned the right to be myself!"

The following is an application filled out by a seventy-five-year-old man. I collected the same application from men who claimed to be sixty-eight, seventy-two, seventy-seven, eighty, eighty-four, and even eighty-nine. All, supposedly, were applying for a job at different large discount stores.

Senior's Application Revealed

NAME: John Doe (or any of the ten other names)

SEX: Not lately, but I am looking for the right woman or one who will at least cooperate.

DESIRED POSITION: President or Vice President. But seriously, I'll take anything. If I was in a position to be picky I wouldn't be applying to this place at all.

DESIRED SALARY: $185,000 a year, plus stock options and a Wall Street-size severance package. If that's not possible, make me an offer and we can discuss.

EDUCATION: Yes

LAST POSITION HELD: As a target for middle-management hostility.

PREVIOUS SALARY: A lot less than I am worth.

REASONS FOR LEAVING: The job sucked.

HOURS AVAILABLE TO WORK: Any

PREFERRED HOURS: 1:30-2:30 p.m., Monday, Tuesday, and Thursday

DO YOU HAVE ANY SPECIAL SKILLS? Yes, but they're better suited to a more intimate environment.

MAY WE CONTACT YOUR CURRENT EMPLOYER? If I had one, would I be filling this out?

DO YOU HAVE ANY PHYSICAL CONDITIONS THAT WOULD PROHIBIT YOU FROM LIFTING UP TO FIFTY POUNDS? Of what?

DO YOU HAVE A CAR? I think the more appropriate question here would be, "Do you have a car that runs?"

In reading the answers to the application, it's easy to notice the sarcasm. There is no need for polite, sometimes, exaggerated answers as in former applications or resumes. He, the "folk old-timer," has been around the proverbial block and experienced the same "work crap" and does not need anything short of honesty. This characteristic of saying whatever to whomever seems to be more a trend reflecting the growing folk culture among seniors. They feel that their age and history allow it. And if you are eighty-nine, who cares? Note, too, the political reference to Wall Street, which echoes many loud grass-roots arguments. There is even bowing to youth slang in some words, like "suck." Combining current trends underscores the strong, enduring outlook of the seniors.

The New Alphabet

In a clever, paradoxical effort at self-effacement, seniors have developed their own alphabet. As they remember the method of learning the A-B-Cs when in grade school, seniors have fun with the "new" alphabet describing "old age," as if they need the memory device. Often younger people define seniors with "memory loss." So seniors counter by "agreeing" with the definition and devising their own methodology. Using humor and stereotypes, seniors are simultaneously affirming their physical changes but mocking the perceptions.

A is for apple, and B is for boat.

> That used to be right, but now it won't float!
> Age before beauty is what we once said.
> But let's be a bit more realistic instead.

A's for arthritis.

B's the bad back.

C's the chest pains, perhaps car-di-ac?

D is for dental decay and decline.

E is for eyesight, can't read that top line!

F is for farting and fluid retention.

G is for gut droop, which I'd rather not mention.

H's high blood pressure, I's rather it low.

J is for joints, out of socket, won't mend.

K is for knees that crack when they bend.

L's for libido, what happened to sex?

M is for memory, I forgot what comes next.

N is for neuralgia, in nerves way down low.

O is for osteo . . . bones that don't grow!

P for prescriptions, I have quite a few, just give me a pill and I'll be good as new!

Q is for queasy. Is it fatal or flu?

R is for reflux, one meal turns to two.

S is for sleepless nights, counting my fears.

T is for Tinnitus; bells in my ears!

U is for urinary; troubles with flow.

V for vertigo, that's "dizzy" you know.

W for worry, now what's going "round"?

X is for X-ray, and what might be found.

Y for another year, I'm left here behind.

Z is for zest I still have in my mind!

In another attempt to reclaim the past, some seniors, in their folk groups, think of interesting new games they can play. Folk games children play have not changed much over the years, so seniors, remembering their "Alley-Alley-Oxen-Free" days, can maintain their gaming spirit with their own folk games. The picture-descriptions are good examples of non-verbal folklore. The following was collected from two nursing homes in St. Louis and from one retirement home. It was posted on bulletin boards.

Pin the toupee on the bald guy.

Twenty questions shouted into your good ear.

Kick the bucket.

Red Rover, Red Rover, the nurse says bend Over.

Simon says something coherent.

Hide and no pee.

Spin the bottle of Mylanta.

Musical recliners.

Sag, you're it.

Seniors Joking

Seniors, in their growing body of lore, continue their self-deprecation with jokes. The universal form of jokes, as used by the baby boomers and seniors, is a clear examples of the way in which the form is the message. The joke/riddle in all its variants helps define the concerns of a folk group—their aspirations, fears, beliefs, perceptions, desires. Seniors, poking fun at themselves, are passing these jokes around through the oral tradition in all their activities throughout the St. Louis area.

A senior citizen said to his eighty-five-year-old friend, "So, you're getting married?"

"Yes, I am," the friend replied.

"Do I know her?"

"No, I don't think so."

"Is she good looking?"

"Not what you would call pretty."

"Is she a good cook?"

"No, she can't cook well at all."

"Does she have a lot of money?"

"No, she lives check to check."

"OK, then, is she good in bed?"

"I really don't know."

"Then, why are you marrying her?"

"Because she can still drive!"

A man was telling his coffee buddy, "I just bought a new hearing aid. Cost me three thousand. But it's perfect; the latest kind."

"Good for you. what kind is it?"

"Eleven-thirty."

An elderly couple was having dinner at their friends' house. After eating, while the wives were in the kitchen, the two men were talking:

"Last night we went out to that new restaurant. Really good."

"What's the name of the restaurant?"

"Oh, what is the name of that flower you give to your girlfriend? You know the one with thorns?"

"You mean a rose?"

"Yes, that's it." He turns around toward the kitchen and says, "Rose, what is the name of the restaurant we went to last night?"

A couple, married sixty-five years, now in their nineties are both having trouble with their memory. The doctor told them that they are OK, but they had better start writing things down to help them remember things.

That night, the man, while they were watching TV, gets up from his chair:

"Want something from the kitchen while I'm up?"

"Yeah, get me a bowl of ice cream."

"Sure," he replies.

"Don't you think you should write it down, so you can remember it, as the doctor told us?" she said.

"No, I can remember it."

"Well, OK, but I'd like some strawberries on top of the ice cream. You'd better write that down."

"Don't be silly. You want a bowl of ice cream with strawberries on top."

"Yeah, and put some whipped cream on the whole thing. Now, write that down!"

Getting angry, he says, "I don't need to write anything down. You want ice cream with strawberries and whipped cream on top. I can remember that!"

Then he goes into the kitchen. Fifteen minutes later he returns to the family room and hands his wife a plate of bacon and eggs.

She stares at the plate.

"Where's my toast?"

A TRIP TO HOME DEPOT DEFINES A MAN'S AGE

And finally, the following story of the "generic" man, which has been printed and passed around many different St. Louis senior groups, captures the essence of "boomer" lore. The history of their aging is recounted and remembered with an all-too-familiar accuracy told in the folk vernacular. Acceptance is the tone of this joke tale with an added implied folk caveat: it's better than the alternative!

You are in the middle of some kind of project around the house—mowing the lawn, putting in a new fence, painting the living room . . . whatever. You are hot and sweaty, covered in dust, lawn clippings, dirt, or paint. You have your old work clothes on. You know the outfit—shorts with the hole in the crotch, old T-shirt with a stain from who knows what, and an old pair of tennis shoes. Right in the middle of this great home improvement project you realize you need to run to Home Depot to get something to help complete the job.

Now, depending on your age, you might do the following:

IN YOUR 20s:

Stop what you are doing. Shave, take a shower, blow-dry your hair, brush your teeth, floss, and put on clean clothes. Check yourself in the mirror and flex. Add a dab of your favorite cologne, because—you never know—you just might meet some hot chick while standing in the checkout lane. Or you went to school with the pretty girl running the register.

IN YOUR 30s:

Stop what you are doing, put on clean shorts and shirt. Change shoes. You married the hot chick so no need for much else. Wash your hands and comb your hair. Check yourself in the mirror. Still got it! Add a shot of your favorite cologne to cover the smell. The cute girl running the register is the kid sister to someone you went to school with.

IN YOUR 40s:

Stop what you are doing. Put on a sweatshirt that is long enough to cover the hole in the crotch of your shorts. Put on different shoes and a hat. Wash your hands. Your bottle of Brute cologne is almost empty so you don't want to waste any of it on a trip to Home Depot. Check yourself in the mirror and do more sucking in than flexing. The hot young thing running the register is your daughter's age and you feel weird thinking she is spicy.

IN YOUR 50s:

Stop what you are doing. Put on a hat; wipe the dirt off your hands and onto your shorts. Change shoes because you don't want to get dog crap in your new sports car. Check yourself in the mirror and you swear not to wear that shirt anymore because it makes you look fat. The cutie running the register smiles when she sees you coming and you think you still have it. Then you remember the hat you have on is from Bubba's Bait and Beer Bar and it says, "I Got Worms."

IN YOUR 60s:

Stop what you are doing. No need for a hat anymore. Hose the dog crap off your shoes. The mirror was shattered when you were in your 50s. You hope you have underwear on so nothing hangs out the hole in your pants. The girl running the register may be cute, but you don't have your glasses on so you are not sure.

IN YOUR 70s:

Stop what you are doing. Wait to go to Home Depot until the drug store has your prescriptions ready, too. You don't even notice the dog crap on your shoes. The young thing at the register stares at you and you realize that your junk is hanging out the hole in your crotch.

IN YOUR 80s:

Stop what you are doing. Start again. Then stop again. Now you remember you need to go to Home Depot. Go to Wal-Mart instead and wander around trying to think what it is you are looking for. Fart out loud and you think someone called out your name. You went to school with the old lady who greeted you at the front door.

What's a home deep hoe? Something for my garden? Where am I? Who am I? Why am I reading this? Did I get it from you? Did you? You farted?

Accurate descriptions? Identifiable? No matter. The folk have spoken! And their reflection on the aging of "a man" is from a perspective never before current in the oral tradition. Underlying is the message: We are all in the same boat!

Getting old has not changed. The difference in the folklore is that the aging process is now celebrated openly. All these examples clearly show the direction of lore of a specific and growing group: retired Americans. They are not fearful of speaking their mind, laughing at themselves, showing that technology is not a scary thing to them, and for "telling it like it is!" There's surely more of their lore as our demographics change! Just keep passing it on.

CHAPTER 7

Occupational Folklore

Perhaps the least understood and most neglected study
in folklore research are the texts related to occupations. Every
occupation is a folk group fulfilling the primary functions of
folklore. They use "folk texts," like their jargon, stories, and beliefs,
even superstitions, to bond, identify with a profession, validate
their lore, and even educate those who wish to join them.

This folklore of the many different occupations does not
include the technical terminology necessary to accomplish a job.
These practices were learned in a formal setting, no doubt, and
must be understood to complete the required task. Nurses, for
example, know the words and practices for their instruments; how
to take blood pressure; how to give injections; how to bathe a
person . . . among many other duties they "officially" learned in
nursing school. It is foundational.

However, as several St. Louis nurse informants have related,
there is lore outside of the technical knowledge. For instance,
one nurse reported that on her floor, when someone dies and
was not expected to die, the nurses tie a knot in one corner of
the bedsheets to keep any more patients from dying. And several
have mentioned the GOMERs in the hospital: Grand Old Men of
the Emergency Room or Get Out of My Emergency Room. These
are people, perhaps homeless, who frequent emergency rooms
of hospitals with various illnesses, mostly fake. The first example
borders on a folk belief, and the second is nursing lore helping to
identify patients and their needs. Neither, of course, was taught
by a professor in nursing school, but their usage is commonly
practiced and recognized. The term or actions are known only by

the nurses as a folk group. This is occupational folklore.

In my book, *You Did What in the Ditch? The Folklore of the American Quilter*, I collected, from hundreds of quilters, examples of the types of folklore that connects them. There is a whole vocabulary, sayings, proverbs, jump rope rhymes, quilt naming, superstitions, and even graffiti associated with the art of quilting. New quilters are expected to know the oral traditions as they learn the craft. If they do not, those in the upper levels of the hierarchy (and there is a hierarchy in quilting!) may not welcome them as easily.

For example, a folk belief held by some quilters is known as the "humility" block. Quilts are a pure folk art where the quilter as folk artist preserves fabric from different sources and cuts the material to form a pattern. Each quilt is identified and the folk name conjures up everlasting folk memories. There is a special heirloom quality to each quilt. But the quilter knows that only God is perfect, so she purposely designs a mistake in every quilt. This mark of humility, in the context of a folk art, recognizes superiority in the exact meaning of a superstition.

This and other lore aids the quilter in bonding and helps identify the folk group as special. Again, the lore were not formally taught, but just evolved from experiences of the quilter over many, many years. Even in the title of the book, "in the ditch," refers to a method of quilting and not a car problem!

The examples which follow were collected and submitted by St. Louisans engaged in the occupation. In many cases, the meanings are not clear, as expected for a folk group. Their communication among themselves has to have some secrecy to it. The members of the folk group, themselves, however, know the meaning of the term or practice, or at least they should.

Also, some of the terms have been adopted by other folk groups just as some of our American words come from other languages. The folk take the word and use it in a variation, which also is a criterion of folklore. In all, the phraseology is learned on the job and is not part of any formal education.

Business

A "Stepford worker" is a person who buys into everything the company says and does.

"Down in the trenches," refers to the working "bees" doing the grunt work or suggesting that managers do the same thing.

"We need to collaborate on the verticals" is becoming more popular in the folk of the business group; no one is certain what it means.

"Let me wrap my head around this" is asking for time to think about something.

"Think outside the box" began in business but now many folk groups use it . . . don't get stuck with the same thinking process; be creative.

"Don't do it. I climbed that same tree myself and got knocked off the branch."

What happened to your idea? "That one fell totally off the vine."

Are you ever told to "keep the bees in the nest?" Do you know what it means?

A new way of meeting another department or company is to have a "grin and grip," which used to be "meet and greet."

"I don't want to do it, but I guess we'll just have to drink the kool-aid." Reference to the mass deaths of Jim Jones religious group in Guyana.

"Get your ducks in a row," and then come and see me. Ever notice a mother duck with her ducklings? Your boss wants order and organization too.

If you are "lost in the sauce," you don't get it or else you have been overlooked.

He has a "10,000 foot view." Is that good or bad?

You've got to "drill down," even though you don't want to. Find the specific risk factor?

We will "peel the onion," to get things moving again. Check every level of the organization.

Let's "circle back around" next week. Meet again to discuss.

"I've got an 'elevator story' if he gets on with me." If the boss gets on the first floor with you and you ride to the tenth, you have something you could tell him in that short period.

We have to "incent" her. A new verb to motivate?

Just go after the "low hanging fruit." Do the easiest task first.

We need a "wet signature." This means no electronic signing would do.

"Why don't we 'cold towel' it until our meeting next week?"

"Slave traders" is another name for people in Human Resources.

When a boss disciplines an employee he doesn't mean to "break his crayons," but he has to do it.

When an employee is not very productive and looks it, he is "screwing the pooch."

When a person wants to have perfect attendance and comes to work with a cold to give to everyone else, he is a "mucus trooper."

Learning this folk vocabulary for business is necessary for the ambitious employee and when mastered he may become a "fast tracker."

When your suggestions are not perceived as good, they are a "warm bowl of nothing."

When the boss wants to take chances with a new policy, he orders everyone to "hang the bell on the cat."

Mandatory meetings, where attendance is taken, to communicate policies, are known as "sheep dip."

When an employee is underperforming, he is moved to another department in a "Muppet Shuffle."

Baseball, Etc.

Baseball, long considered America's pastime, has contributed many phrases to our folk vocabulary. Its language can be found in all folk groups, with different applications. "Ball park figure," "bush league," "MVP," "home run," "hit it out of the park," "grand slam," "ahead in the count," "clean-up hitter," and "big league" among many others. Often the baseball words appear in casual conversation among friends and it is not difficult to understand the meaning. The learning curve is not a big one as the terms are part of our culture.

Other sports contribute terms also to our conversation. Just think of "slam dunk," "ace," "bagel," "mulligan," "come out fighting," "hit below the belt," "nothing but net," "power play," "he plays above the rim," "he can't turn the corner," "bring your A-game," "gut check time," or even "crunch time."

But beyond the folk terminology, athletes often live by ritual and folk beliefs. Winning is important and they prepare as well as they can, but for that extra edge, they "have" to do something. Rituals develop into sports superstitions. As the ancients knocked on trees to bow to the gods, and we "knock on wood" so athletes follow their acts for "fear of the gods," to give them that extra edge for victory.

From interviews with some St. Louis Cardinals in the locker room and from other professional athlete informants, these superstitions add a dimension to occupational folklore.

BASEBALL

Never step on the base lines when going on or off the field during a game; bad luck.

Never loan your bat to anyone; certain jinx.

During a no-hit game, never talk about it in the dugout; it will be jinxed and never be completed.

When first going on to the field when the game starts, place both feet on each step of the dugout.

Eat the same food at every meal before every game. If a team loses, eat a different meal for every meal until they win gain.

If a player is in a slump, he might take his bat to bed with him.

Wearing the same T-shirt under your uniform, no matter how ragged or how dirty. Washing it will jinx the game.

Run around the bases, stomping on each bag, before the game starts.

"Rally" caps, baseball caps turned inside out for good luck, are displayed both by players in the dugout and fans in the stands.

The "Rally Squirrel," which appeared at Busch Stadium during the 2011 World Series has become a legend in the area. Some fans attribute the unlikely victory of the Series to the squirrel. Game Six of the contest was the proof, as they say!

Never cross hockey sticks; very bad luck.

Never wear yellow when playing tennis . . . bad luck.

When fishing, spit on your bait before casting. (Spittle is a popular "charm" in many superstitions as the ancients believed that spittle was the actual spirit of the person and was a cure-all; even if put on a broken mirror it would void the seven years of bad luck.)

Tap the goalie on the shin before every game in order to win the hockey contest.

Never keep the first fish you catch. Throw it back into the water.

Never step on the lines of the court when starting a tennis match.

Bounce the ball at least three times before taking a foul shot in basketball. (Here, the number three is used again and is a "magical" number in much of folklore.)

Always wear a double number on your uniform if a football player.

Don't tell anyone how many fish you've caught before you are done; you'll catch no more after telling.

When golfing, don't use any balls with a number higher than three.

At the end of the warm-up in a basketball game, the last person to make a basket will have a good game.

Some athletes wear their underwear inside out for good luck and to protect them from injury.

During a shut-out in a hockey game, never mention it to the goalie, or don't even go near the goalie as to be accused of jinxing him and the score.

There are many more superstitions and game-time rituals specific to a certain athlete. More than folk vocabulary is part of their culture. Athletes are under pressure to win. A lot of money is at stake. If wearing the same socks for every contest works, why not keep doing it?

Nurses

Nurses, too, not surprisingly, have their own folklore. On a daily basis they deal with life-and-death situations. This strain requires a language, including acronyms that must be recognized STAT. But nurses, within their own group, as an excellent example of "folk bonding," often use "Mash-like humor" to ease their stress. As with other folk and occupational groups, nurses try to define themselves in their own terms. The popular, "You Know You're a . . . whatever," formula tale is a good example of nurses' lore. (See St. Louisan, Hoosier, or Bosnian definitions in other sections of my research.)

The following was sent to me by two nurses from two different St. Louis hospitals. Given the universality of the profession and the standardized education, this nurses' lore is not specific to St. Louis, except for a few examples, perhaps. But the list is a good example of the many forms of lore that folk groups have. Nurses have a folk vocabulary and are sometimes superstitious. This is another important example of their body of folklore.

YOU KNOW YOU'RE A NURSE WHEN . . .

> You refer to motorcyclists as organ donors.

You ever told a patient he didn't need to be dead to donate an organ.

You have seen more moons than the Hubble telescope.

You no longer have a gag reflex.

You believe if it's wet and sticky and not yours, leave it alone.

You own at least three pens with the names of prescription medications on them.

You wash your hands before you go to the bathroom.

You hope there's a special place in hell for the inventor of the call light.

Discussing dismemberment during a meal is perfectly normal.

You believe you have patients who are demonically possessed.

You believe chocolate is a food group.

You know it's a full moon without looking at the sky.

You've ever had a patient with a nose ring, a tongue piercing, and ten earring holes say, "I'm afraid of shots."

Eating microwave popcorn out of a clean bedpan is perfectly normal.

You believe that "shallow gene pool" should be a recognized medical diagnosis.

You invent a new game called, "Specimen, specimen, who's got the specimen?"

You believe that Prozac should be in an aerial spray.

You get the strong urge to stand and wolf down your food

even in the nicest restaurants.

You think pizza, cookies, and coke make a balanced meal.

You use the term "turn and baste" and you are nowhere near a kitchen.

You've had a patient look you in the eye and say, "I don't know how that got stuck in there. I don't even like zucchini."

You think it's acceptable to use "penis" and "vagina" in normal conversation.

You consider a tongue depressor an eating utensil.

You believe that "too stupid to live" should be a medical diagnosis.

You believe that the "on-call nurse" program is a satanic plot.

You've ever thought that a blood pressure cuff would be a great Christmas gift.

You've ever held a 14-gauge needle over a patient and said, "You are just going to feel a little stick."

The list could go on with many more examples given all that is involved in the career of nursing. Many, in fact, are created in nursing groups during breaks or in other social gatherings. They can continue to bond outside of their "temple," and validate their work. If they chose, also, they could speak in acronyms so others would not understand—a perfect example of a folk group tactic.

Lawyers

Lawyers are, probably, the only occupational group that has ever had a grass roots movement against its "folk" practices. During the 1970s and even endorsed by President Carter, "The Plain

English" movement was an attempt to "demand" that attorneys use simple language so that the lay person could understand the document or the decision. Many lawyers and more judges even agreed with the purpose of the movement and joined the cause.

For hundreds of years, lawyers have been accused of using mysterious language to guarantee work and to "give them the old razzle-dazzle," as the song pokes fun. Stilted language and foreign phrases, spoken as a dialect, was regularly cursed as unnecessary. It's a folk vocabulary clearly identifying the folk group, but tradition, another criterion of folklore, is paramount. Legal jargon has been so well established for centuries that the language must be taught in order to be accepted into the practice through an examination. It is the "folk" language for the attorney and must often be trusted by the layperson. "Obiter dictum," "pro bono," "pro per," or "corpus delecti," may be heard on a television program about lawyers, but the common folk rarely use the terms in their conversations. This is a different slant on the folk vocabulary of the group. Lawyers, arguably, need "their" language.

So, the folk, who believe themselves at the mercy of the legal profession, respond as they often do. They can do nothing about getting "plain language," but they can joke about it! And they have and continue to make "legal fun."

As stated, lawyers must use their jargon; the profession demands it. So in a self-deprecating way, they welcome jokes about their speech. In fact, there are entire jokelore research studies on lawyer jokes alone. Happily, many of the jokes have been contributed by lawyers themselves. Following are some of the jokes that also serve as examples of the kind of lore that occupations can include. Note that some "actual" court discussions are opportunities for lawyers to laugh at the rest of us who don't understand "plain English." They seem to say that even if we changed our jargon to "your" language, you wouldn't understand anyway.

YOU ARE IN A ROOM WITH A MASS MURDERER, AND A TERRORIST. YOUR GUN ONLY HAS TWO BULLETS. WHAT DO YOU DO?

Shoot the lawyer twice.

WHAT HAPPENS WHEN A LAWYER TAKES VIAGRA?

He gets taller.

HOW MANY LAWYERS DOES IT TAKE TO CHANGE A LIGHT BULB?

How many can you afford?

WHY DID GOD MAKE SNAKES JUST BEFORE LAWYERS?

Just to practice.

WHY WON'T SHARKS ATTACK LAWYERS?

Professional courtesy.

WHAT DO YOU THROW TO A DROWNING LAWYER?

His partners.

WHAT DO YOU CALL TWENTY LAWYERS BURIED UP TO THEIR CHINS IN CEMENT?

Not enough cement.

WHAT DOES A LAWYER USE FOR BIRTH CONTROL?

His personality.

WHAT HAPPENS WHEN YOU CROSS A PIG WITH A LAWYER?

Nothing; there are some things a pig won't do.

How many lawyer jokes are there?

only three; the rest are true.

WHAT'S THE DIFFERENCE BETWEEN GOD AND A LAWYER?
God doesn't think he's a lawyer.

WHAT'S THE DIFFERENCE BETWEEN AN ACCOUNTANT AND A LAWYER?
Accountants know they are boring.

WHY WAS THE LAWYER READING THE BIBLE RIGHT BEFORE HE DIED?
He was looking for loopholes.

COURTROOM DIALOGUE

Lawyer: What is your date of birth?

Witness: July 22.

Lawyer: What year?

Witness: Every year.

Lawyer: So you were gone until you returned?

Lawyer: So you were alone or by yourself?

Lawyer: Your son, the 21-year-old, how old is he?

Lawyer: Were you present in the court this morning when you were sworn in?

Lawyer: You don't know what it was or what it looked like, but can you describe it?

Lawyer: Now, doctor, isn't it true that when a person dies in his sleep he just passes away quietly and doesn't know about it until the next morning?

And of course, since the folk poke fun at lawyers, and they know we will need them at some point, they tell us how to tell if we need a new lawyer:

Giggles every time he hears the word "briefs."

Picks the jury by playing "duck-duck-goose."

Is seen by the prosecutors and they high-five each other.

Tries to sell you Amway during your first meeting

Asks a hostile witness to "pull my finger."

Begins closing arguments with "as Ally McBeal says . . ."

Every time his objection is overruled, he says, "whatever."

You definitely need a new lawyer!

All the examples of occupations lore presented are certainly not exhaustive. The nurses, doctors, businessmen, athletes, and lawyers are among the occupations with the most folklore attached to them. They are represented in vocabulary, jokes, self-deprecating lore, folk beliefs, superstitions, rituals, and in folk terms adapted by the mainstream. Much more research is necessary to understand the full character of their lore. What does it say about our culture that we tell lawyer jokes? The superstitions of baseball players . . . surprising? Silly? All the buzzwords from the world of business . . . any wonder if any work gets done. Nurses poking fun at themselves and patients . . . validation? Are all just symptomatic of the general culture? What folk vocabulary is part of occupations you are familiar with? How are they learned and passed on? Do your "folk" try to keep their lore secret and "above you"?

The folk can and are being affected in many different ways by the lore of various occupations. It's important to collect it, preserve it, and figure out how it applies and reflects our culture.

CHAPTER 8

Is the Computer Male or Female?

The oral tradition is the basic focus of folklore and folkways. We hear a joke or a story or a legend and tell someone who tells someone else and on and on. In the telling, the folk text might be changed, however slightly, to reflect the culture of the teller or the audience. These examples of lore have been the primary focus for the scholar-collector. The computer has added another dimension.

All the topics reflected in the "passing on" of folklore continue to flourish via the computer but are received and passed on at lightning speed. An example of folklore collected in St. Louis and about St. Louis can be sent worldwide immediately with variations making them appear indigenous to the region. But the universality of the theme is important to document for interpreting a culture.

The proverbial "battle of the sexes" has always been a part of folklore primarily in joke form. The "dumb blonde" and the clueless "Dagwood" are stock figures in stories and tales. And the "battle" continues in clever folk "forms" aided by an aging population who have the time to reflect and create. The stereotypes are still present but the emphasis on roles, if read carefully, has changed the argument.

Consider the following examples of the new forms of folklore. All were collected from St. Louis informants either in group settings or personal interviews. Senior citizen residences, retirement "villages," "Over-50" clubs, bingo, poker, or bunko nights are all fertile ground for collection. Often the material is passed around leading to brisk, lively conversation, and then passed on through endless computer contact lists.

The Feminist Interview

One day a laundry-challenged husband decided to wash his T-shirt. Soon after he got to the laundry room, he yelled to his wife, "What setting do I use on the washing machine?" "It depends," she answered. "What does it say on your shirt?" He yelled back, "Ohio State." And blondes are dumb?

A couple is lying in bed. The man says, "I'm going to make you the happiest woman in the world." The wife says, "I'll miss you."

"It's just too hot to wear clothes today," Bob says as he steps out of the shower. "What do you think the neighbors would say if I mowed the lawn like this?" "Probably that I married you for your money."

Dear Lord, I pray for wisdom to understand my man. Love to forgive him. Patience for his moods. Because, Lord, if I pray for strength, I'll beat him to death. Amen.

Why do little boys whine?
They are practicing to be men.

What do you call a handcuffed man?
Trustworthy.

What does it mean when a man in your bed is gasping for breath and calling your name?
You did not hold the pillow down long enough.

What do you call an intelligent, good-looking, sensitive man?

A rumor.

Why do men whistle when they are sitting on the toilet? It helps them remember which end to wipe.

How do you keep your husband from reading your emails? Rename the folder, "Instruction Manuals."

While creating husbands, God promised women that good and ideal husbands would be found in all corners of the world. Then He made the earth round!

The history of the woman in America has been one of reform and resistance. In American folklore this theme has been reflected in dumb blonde jokes, Little Audrey Jokes, corset rhymes and tales, and even anti-feminist graffiti. Underlying all was the superiority of the sexes. In computer lore, the woman gets her place redefined.

Women and Wine

Women are like apples on trees. The best ones are at the top of the tree. Most men don't want to reach for the good ones because they are afraid of falling and getting hurt. Instead, they sometimes take the apples from the ground that aren't as good, but easy. The apples at the top think something is wrong with them, when in reality, they're amazing. They just have to wait for the right man to come along, the one who is brave enough to climb all the way to the top of the tree.

Now, men . . . men are like fine wine. They begin as grapes, and it's up to women to stomp the shit out of them until they turn into something acceptable to have dinner with.

Share this with all the good apples you know.

Note the moralistic tone of the tale. Women acknowledge that "other" women might be "bad" but acceptable to men, all for the wrong reasons. But the gullible men don't want to get "hurt" . . .

double meaning? In trying to find the "good" wife, so character-istically, they "settle." But even if men find the "top-of-the-tree apple" they still have to be shaped for "proper" behavior.

Lastly, there is a plea to share the tale with women "apples" who get it!

But the lore continues, transmitted from the "good" woman. They even encourage all women to send this to men just to annoy them!

Men: The Problem

Ever notice how all of women's problems start with MEN?

MENtal illness

MENstrual cramps

MENtal breakdown

MENopause

GUYnecologist

And where there is REAL trouble:

HISterectomy

Send this to ALL MEN just to annoy them!

But the plan of attack does not stop with this. Women "con-cede" that men are happier and why not? Here's the folk answer:

WHY MEN ARE JUST HAPPIER PEOPLE

What do you expect from such simple creatures?

Your last name stays put.

The garage is all yours.

Wedding plans take care of themselves.

Chocolate is just another snack.

You can be president.

You can wear a white T-shirt to a water park.

Car mechanics tell you the truth.

The world is your urinal.

Wrinkles add character.

People never stare at your chest while talking to you.

New shoes don't cut, mangle, or blister your feet.

One mood, *all* the time.

A five-day vacation requires only one suitcase.

Your underwear is $7.95 for a three-pack.

The same hairstyle lasts for years, or decades!

One wallet, one pair of shoes, one color, all seasons.

You can "do" your nails with a pocketknife.

You can do Christmas shopping for 30 relatives on December 24, in 45 minutes.

Wedding dress: $3,000; tuxedo rental: $100.

But the battle continues. Men want to stay in combat mode and get more volunteers. Their weapon is the folk text, the joke. At least they think it is!

WHY IS A LAUNDROMAT A REALLY BAD PLACE TO PICK UP A WOMAN?
Because a woman who can't even afford a washing machine will probably never be able to support you.

WHY DO WOMEN HAVE SMALLER FEET THAN MEN?
It's one of those "evolutionary things" that allows them to stand closer to the kitchen sink.

HOW DO YOU KNOW WHEN A WOMAN IS ABOUT TO SAY SOMETHING SMART?
When she starts a sentence with, "A man once told me . . ."

HOW DO YOU FIX A WOMAN'S WATCH?
You don't; there is a clock on the oven.

WHY DO MEN FART MORE THAN WOMEN?
Because woman can't shut up long enough to build up the required pressure.

IF THE DOG IS BARKING AT THE BACK DOOR AND YOUR WIFE IS YELLING AT THE FRONT DOOR, WHO DO YOU LET IN FIRST?
The dog, of course. He'll shut up once you let him in.

WHY DO MEN DIE BEFORE THEIR WIVES?
They want to.

ORDER: SEND THIS TO GOOD MEN WHO KNOW THE TRUTH!

How many men does it take to open a beer?

None, It should be opened when she brings it.

The men's argument keeps the woman in the home working for him. And he's boss enough to believe that he is speaking the truth by again pleading that the message be sent to other men to get more troops for the battle. The folk theme continues.

A new argument has entered the folklore of the sexes: retirement. If the woman maintains her role as homemaker and if the man retires and stays at home, what happens to the organizational schedule of the woman? Changing demographics over the past two decades, advances in medicine, more research in health lifestyles have all contributed to us living longer. So the new arrangement, post-retirement, requires new rules. Or does it? Here's some advice from Bob who really understands women!

Advice from Bob, a Retired Husband

(Letter to the editor)

It is important for men to remember that, as women grow older, it becomes harder for them to maintain the same quality of housekeeping as when they were younger. When you notice this, try not to yell at them. Some are oversensitive, and there's nothing worse than an oversensitive woman.

My name is Bob. Let me relate how I handled the situation with my wife. When I retired last year, it became necessary for Dotty to get a full-time job, along with her part-time job, both for extra income and for the health benefits that we needed. Shortly after she started working, I noticed that she was beginning to show her age. I usually get home from the golf club about the same time she gets home from work.

Although she knows how hungry I am, she almost always says she has to rest for half an hour or so before she starts dinner. I don't yell at her. Instead, I tell her to take her time and just wake me when she gets dinner on the table. I generally have lunch at the golf club, so eating out is not reasonable. I'm ready for some home-cooked grub when I hit the door. She used to do the dishes as soon as we finished eating. But now, it's not unusual for them to sit on the table for several hours after dinner.

I do what I can by diplomatically reminding her several times each evening that they won't clean themselves. I know she really appreciates this, as it does seem to motivate her to get them done before she goes to bed.

Another symptom of aging is complaining, I think. For example, she will say that it is difficult for her to find time to pay the monthly bills during her lunch hour. But, Boys, we take 'em for better or worse, so I just smile and offer encouragement. I tell her to stretch it out over two or even three days. That way, she won't have to rush so much. I also remind her that missing lunch completely now and then wouldn't hurt her any (if you know what I mean!). I like to think tact is one of my strong points.

When doing simple jobs, she seems to think she needs more rest periods. She had to take a break when she was only half-finished mowing the yard. I try not to make a scene. I'm a fair man. I tell her to fix herself a nice, big, cold glass of freshly squeezed lemonade and just sit for a while, and, as long as she is making one for herself, she may as well make one for me, too.

I know that I probably look like a saint in the way I support my wife. I'm not saying that showing this much consideration is easy. Many men will find it difficult. Some will find it impossible. Nobody knows better than I do how frustrating women get as they get older. However, Guys, even if you just use a little more tact and less criticism of your aging wife because of this notice, I will consider that writing it was well worthwhile. After all, we are put on this earth to help each other.

NOTE: Bob died suddenly on June 30 of a perforated rectum. The police report said he was found with a Calloway extra-long fifty-inch Big Bertha Driver II golf club jammed up his rear end, with barely five inches of grip showing and a sledgehammer lying nearby. His wife was arrested and charged with murder. The all-woman jury took only ten minutes to find her Not Guilty, accepting her defense that Bob, somehow without looking, accidentally sat down on his own golf club.

Of course, it's not difficult to note the convoluted logic and the conceit of the writer. The exaggeration is overstating the importance and superiority of men. But Dotty triumphs in the end. (No pun intended). She is judged, understandably, by her pure peers and the battle continues and becomes a war . . . folklore aided by the computer.

Once married, however, another theme develops and becomes a constant folk text: fighting. Often, it becomes a war of wits, inevitable and caustic, and it keeps "passing on."

And then the Fight Started . . .

My wife was hinting about what she wanted for our upcoming anniversary. She said, "I want something shiny that goes from 0 to 150 in about three seconds." I bought her a bathroom scale.
AND THEN THE FIGHT STARTED . . .

My wife sat down next to me as I was flipping channels. She asked, "What's on TV?" I said, "Dust."
AND THEN THE FIGHT STARTED . . .

My wife was standing nude, looking in the bedroom mirror. She was not happy with what she saw and said to me, "I feel horrible. I look old, fat, and ugly. I really need you to pay me a compliment." I replied, "Your eyesight's damn near perfect."
AND THEN THE FIGHT STARTED . . .

I took my wife to a restaurant. The waiter, for some reason, took my order first. "I'll have the rib eye, rare, please." The waiter said, "Aren't you worried about the mad cow?" "Nah, she can order for herself."
AND THEN THE FIGHT STARTED . . .

My wife and I were sitting at a table at her high school reunion, and she kept staring at a drunken man swigging his drink as he sat alone at a nearby table. I asked her, "Do you know him?" "Yes," she sighed. "He's my old boyfriend. I understand he took to drinking right after we split up those many years ago and I hear he hasn't been sober since." "My God," I said, "Who would think a person could go on celebrating that long?"
AND THEN THE FIGHT STARTED . . .

After retiring, I went to the Social Security Office to apply for Social Security. The woman behind the counter asked me for my driver's license to verify my age. I looked in my pockets and realized that I had left my wallet at home. I told the woman that I was very sorry, but I would have to go home and come back later. The woman said, "Unbutton your shirt." So I opened my shirt revealing my silver hair. She said, "That silver hair on your chest is proof enough for me," and processed my application. When I got home, I excitedly told my wife about my experience. She said, "You should have dropped your pants. You might have gotten disability, too."
AND THEN THE FIGHT STARTED . . .

This constant game of one-upmanship has long been a staple of folk texts. Who wins the battles or war? Who is superior? Who cares? Maybe the bantering is expected in a marriage. Maybe the jabs are bonding. Maybe the marriage is resigned. Maybe, why? Because the folk keep passing them on and on and on.

A recent collected text from a group of retired men, however, seems to suggest that the game of man vs. woman is very simple: make her happy. They have started passing on some "Rules" for men and it applies to all "Gentlemen."

The Demerit System

In the world of romance, one single thing matters: make the woman happy.

Do something she likes and you get points. Do something she dislikes and points are subtracted. You don't get any points for something she expects. No complaints: that's the way the game is played. It's time to accept!

Here is a guide to the points system:

SIMPLE DUTIES

You make the bed. (+1)

You make the bed but forget the decorative pillows. (0)

You throw the bedspread over the rumpled sheets. (-1)

GIFTS

You go out to buy her what she wants (+5) in the rain. (+8)

But return with beer. (-5)

PROTECTIVE DUTIES

You check out a suspicious noise at night. (+1)

You check out a suspicious noise and it is nothing. (0)

You check out a suspicious noise and it is something. (+5)

You pummel it with an iron rod. (+10)

It's her pet dog. (-20)

You stay by her side for the entire party. (0)

You stay by her side for a while, then leave to chat with an old school friend. (-2)

Named Candy. (-10)

Candy is a dancer. (-20)

Candy has implants. (-80)

HER BIRTHDAY

You take her out to dinner. (+2)

You take her out to dinner and it's not a sports bar. (+3)

Okay, it's a sports bar. (-2)

And it's all-you-can-eat night. (-3)

It's a sports bar, all-you-can-eat night, and your face is painted the colors of your favorite team. (-10)

A NIGHT OUT

You take her to a movie. (+1)

You take her to a movie she likes. (+3)

You take her to a movie you hate. (+6)

You take her to a movie you like. (-2)

It's called *Death Cop.* (-3)

You lied and said it was a foreign film about orphans. (-15)

You develop a noticeable potbelly. (-15)

You develop a noticeable potbelly and exercise to get rid of it. (+10)

You develop a noticeable potbelly and resort to baggy jeans and baggy Hawaiian shirts. (-30)

You say, "It doesn't matter; you have one, too." (-8000)

THE BIG QUESTION

She asks, "Do I look fat?" (-5)

(Yes, you lose points here, no matter what.)

You hesitate in responding. (-10)

You reply, "Where?" (-35)

You give any other response. (-20)

COMMUNICATION

When she wants to talk about a problem, you listen, displaying what looks like a concerned expression? (0)

You listen, for over 30 minutes. (+50)

You listen for more than 30 minutes without looking at TV. (+500)

She realizes this is because you have fallen asleep. (-4000)

OK, now there are rules for the battle of the sexes. But did the man surrender? And did he really "get it" after he got much older? And is the beginning a plea to end the jabs? The advice at the beginning: Gentlemen, remember it well! . . . warning or more warfare? Note the folk themes throughout the number system: men sleeping during conversation with women; women worrying about their size; women's need for partnering; women really setting the rules of morals and etiquette; men oblivious to the needs of a woman. All these are folk memes present in all examples of lore. The war will continue aided by the computer!

But recent lore seems to have reached a truce. Acclaimed by the folk, there should be two dictionaries for the sexes and a new form of communication distinguishing, "he said," and "she said."

Words with Different Meanings for the Sexes

THINGY (THING-EE), N.

Female: any part under a car's hood

Male: the strap fastener on a woman's bra

COMMUNICATION: (KO-MYOO-NI-KAY-SHOUN), N.

Female: the open sharing of thoughts and feelings with one's partner

Male: leaving a note before taking off on a fishing trip with the boys

ENTERTAINMENT: (EN-TER-TAYN-MENT), N.

Female: a good movie, concert, play, or book

Male: anything that can be done while drinking beer

MAKING LOVE: (MAY-KING LUV), N.

Female: the greatest expression of intimacy a couple can achieve

Male: call it whatever you want, just as long as we do it

Taking a Risk
Female:
fully opening up one's
self emotionally to another

Taking a Risk
Male:
playing football without
a cup

COMMITMENT: (KO-MIT-MENT), N.

Female: a desire to get married and raise a family

Male: trying not to hit on other women while out with the wife or girlfriend

FLATULENCE: (FLAT-U-LENS), N.

Female: an embarrassing by-product of indigestion

Male: a source of entertainment, self-expression, and male bonding

REMOTE CONTROL: (RI-MOHT KON-TROHL), N.

Female: a device for changing from one TV channel to another

Male: a device for scanning through all four hundred channels every five minutes

Two informants told me that the pronunciation guide was for men!

Two-Way Dialogue (Not the Woman Alone!) for the Sexes

HE SAID: "I don't know why you wear a bra; you've got nothing to put in it."

SHE SAID: "You wear pants don't you?"

HE SAID: "Shall we try swapping positions tonight?"

SHE SAID: "That's a good idea. You stand by the ironing board while I sit on the sofa and fart."

HE SAID: "What have you been doing with all the grocery money I gave you?"

SHE SAID: "Turn sideways and look in the mirror."

HE SAID: "Why don't women blink during sex?"

SHE SAID: "They don't have time."

HE SAID: "How many men does it take to change a roll of toilet paper?"

SHE SAID: "We don't know; it's never happened."

SHE SAID: "Why is it difficult to find men who are sensitive, caring, and good looking?"

HE SAID: "They already have boyfriends."

SHE SAID: "What do you call a woman who knows where her husband is every night?"

HE SAID: "A widow."

<u>HE SAID:</u> "Why are married women heavier than single women?"

<u>SHE SAID:</u> "Single women come home, see what's in the fridge and go to bed. Married women come home, see what's in the bed, and go to the fridge."

St. Louis women often pass this dialogue around at bachelorette parties to "inform" the soon-to-be bride. It's women's role in counseling: mothering, being *mom*, moralistic, and a warning. The humor is apparent, but the meaning and stereotypes are deeper in the attempt to reach compromises. Undoubtedly, the newest lore about the sexes is still to circulate in the never-ending folk war.

CHAPTER 9

St. Louis Irish

The contributions of the Irish to the culture and history of St. Louis is, arguably, greater and longer rooted than any other ethnic group. Excellent histories have well documented how the Irish arrived in St. Louis near its founding, expanded their presence in the early nineteenth century, and cemented their footprints as solid and productive citizens. The St. Louis Irish were traders, merchants, shopkeepers, laborers, policemen, politicians, entrepreneurs, priests, nuns, preachers, philanthropists, patrons of the arts, teachers, publishers, firemen, bar tenders, and even entertainers among other occupations. And in many of these professions, the Irish established the templates for decades and decades of St. Louis practices and development.

When one considers all that the Irish have concretely contributed to the culture that is St. Louis, the list can be staggering. Much of their contribution is concretely visible in the structures they built, like churches, or in the hospitals they established, or in the sense of social service they fostered, or in the pattern of politics they established, or in the effective educational curricula under their tutelage. Paradoxically, these superior achievements, with tangents everywhere, speak of very little related to folklore. The oral traditions of the Irish are difficult to document.

When talking with many informants who are proudly Irish, it was clear that the pattern of assimilation by their ancestors in St. Louis, and carried on by them was the most important element to remember. They were Americans! As English-language speakers, the Irish found it easier to assimilate and run, not walk, into their new life. They eagerly did and often abandoned the lore—not forgetting it, but not using it readily.

Try free association with the Irish. Using the terms "Irish in St. Louis," what comes to your mind immediately? Green, St. Patrick's Day, corned beef and cabbage, shamrocks, leprechauns, Jameson and Guinness, perhaps, Blarney Stone, Irish jig, Catholicism, nuns and rulers, drunkards, blessings, Dogtown, pubs, potatoes, even snakes? There are surely more, but the folklore question: do these associations apply to Irish in other American cities? Certainly! So where is the St. Louis–style Emerald Isle?

Perhaps a tale from John Corbett, from the famous Corbett family, in Dogtown, can explain: "Mary Gallagher, an elderly Irish immigrant, was a frequent visitor at the pub as she was raised in the Irish pub culture way of life. Occasionally, my parents, Bob and Louise Corbett, would take the kids to the tavern on Saturday afternoon to get lunch. The previous evening my brother and I went to the show to see the movie, *Darby O'Gill and the Little People*. So the next day while we were having lunch at the Pilot House, Mary was sitting in her favorite stool at the bar and I asked her a silly questions. "Mary, do you believe in the 'little people'"? Mary answered in her heavy Irish brogue. "I don't believe in the little people—but they're there." I studied her answer as the fellow bar patrons laughed loudly."

That's the paradox. There is an Irish culture in folklore in St. Louis, just keep digging and do more fieldwork. Go back to the Irish informants and give them examples of lore to spark their minds. It worked! Much of the words from a free association exercise about Irish were part of some folk type or folk genre most St. Louis Irish knew. But as their ancestors, they were not eager to admit any "serious" practicing. To paraphrase old Mary Gallagher, the lore is everywhere, but be careful how you pass it on!

So, what follows is "organized random" St. Louis Irish folklore. Many familiar texts, identified in the study of folklore, are, not surprisingly, part of the folkways of the group. As any ethnic identity, the Irish follow the patterns of familiar lore. But, except on St. Patrick's Day, keep them quietly and sacredly in your Irish soul! Bob Corbett, the generous and knowledgeable "mayor of Dogtown," (my title) told me in one of our interviews: "Three things are important to the Irish: the Church (Catholic), family, and friendship." Think of all three as you consider the folklore which follows.

You Know You're Irish When . . .

(Go to any Irish pub in St. Louis and these descriptions won't stop.)

You swear very, very well.

You will never play professional basketball.

You don't remember the words to a song; perhaps you never knew them, but you sing anyway.

You cannot keep a secret; it's not part of an Irish person's DNA.

You have no idea how to make a long story short, but you start out by saying you do!

You have sisters or cousins named Mary, Eileen, Bridget, and at least one relative will be Mary Eileen Bridget!

You have Irish Alzheimer's; you forget everything but the grudges.

You have at least two relatives who are not speaking to each other. They are not fighting, lad, they are just not speaking to each other!

You met your wife in a pub.

You met your accountant in a pub.

You met your best friend in a pub.

You met your lawyer in a pub.

You met your future brother-in-law in a pub.

You met your first girlfriend in a pub.

You met your future father-in-law in a pub.

You have at least one aunt who is a nun.

You have at least one uncle who is a priest.

You know someone named "Murph" or "Mac."

You don't think there is a huge different between losing your temper and killing someone.

You are not sure there is a God, but you are deadly certain that the Pope is infallible.

You don't have to study for tests because your mother lit a candle for you at mass.

You think St. Patrick's Day is *the* major holiday of the year.

You think that a lite beer is punishment from God.

You respect the truth but use it only in emergencies.

You believe that to forgive is divine, but it does not apply to you.

You think that stirring the bubbles out of a coke cures all illnesses.

You always see leprechauns after the pub closes and often times they are twins.

You can't get a tan no matter what you do, even from a tanning booth!

You can't wait for the other guy to stop talking so you can start talking.

These delightful, self-effacing stereotypes help define the Irish culture. The transmission of the definitions *within* the culture is acceptable, so, again, be careful!

Irish Sayings: Proverbs, Blessings, and Toasts

Proverbs are the folk wisdom of any culture. In a simple, declarative sentence, the metaphor speaks proverbial volumes. The meaning, content, and tone are clues to the nature of the folk who speak them. Proverbs are easily transmitted and passed to all members of the culture and often retain their specific words without variants. However the different versions do appear in other ethnicities. It will be evident in these folk expressions from Irish informants.

Put silk on a goat and it's still a goat. (Remember the lipstick on a pig tag line in national elections?)

The well-fed man does not understand the lean man.

If you have a name for rising early you can stay in bed till mid morning.

No matter how tall your grandfather was, you have to do your own growing.

Necessity knows no law.

The wearer of the shoes knows best where they pinch.

Both your friend and your enemy think that you will not die.

A trout in the pot is better than a salmon in the river.

Don't bless the fish till it gets on the land.

Loud cackle, little egg.

The shallowest water makes the most noise.

A wise woman is better than a foolish doctor.

You can't make a racehorse out of a donkey.

A wild goose never laid a tame egg.

He who conquers himself conquers an enemy.

If someone comes with a gossip story to you, he will bring two away with him.

Death is the poor man's doctor.

Nobody knows where his sod of death is.

Never take a wife who has no fault.

Praise the bridge you walk over.

If you wait long enough for the ferry you will get over at last.

Never sell your hen on a wet day.

Say little, but the little you say, say well.

However long the road, there will come a turning.

There are three things without rule: a pig, a mule, and a woman.

The old person is a child twice.

A fire, a flood, and a falsehood are the fastest things in the world.

If it's known to three people it is not a secret.

Referring to Irish guests: Like Abbey's Irish rose, will stay as long as wanted.

BLESSINGS

Arguably, the most popular or recognized of Irish folk vocabulary is the blessing. They are usually soft, romantic, future-oriented that wish only the best for someone. Very often they are spoken at rites of passage, especially at weddings or wedding anniversaries. Many view them as having the same purpose of autograph book verses which are inscribed as someone "graduates" to a new unknown life. In later years they can be remembered and reflected upon. They even become a "permanent" lore as the blessings appear on all manner of decoration.

The paradox of Irish lore in St. Louis does, curiously, not relate to these blessings. Informants carefully and enthusiastically recount family occasions where they were spoken.

May good fortune be yours and may your joys never end.

May your blessings outnumber shamrocks.

May God and the Virgin Mary take the harm of the year away from you.

May the light of heaven shine on your grave.

May you be in Heaven a half hour before the Devil knows you're dead. (This is the most popular blessing from Irish informants.)

As you slide down the banister of life may the splinters never point in the wrong direction. (This is a very popular autograph book verse in St. Louis folklore.)

May you have warm words on a cold evening, a full moon on a dark night, and the road downhill all the way to your door.

May you be as happy as the flowers in May.

TOASTS

Toasts are intimately connected to Irish lore. They fit the stereotype of "pub life" and can be used for any occasion. Often an Irish person, during a regular, customary drinking session, will stand up and toast his friends and even the whole crowd.

Sometimes the toasts are crude, sometimes romantic, sometimes devilish, often said in verse, or combined with a blessing but they always define the Irish culture everywhere. Another necessary component of a toast: a drink! Beer is the strong preference. In fact, there are those who believe that the wishes of a toast will not occur if one is not drinking an Irish beer! So from morning to night toasts can be offered.

Here's health and prosperity
To you and all posterity
And them that doesn't drink with sincerity
That they may be damned for all eternity!

To living one hundred years with one extra year to repent.

May you get all your wishes but one so that you have something to strive for.

Health and long life to you
The woman of your choice to you
A child every year to you
Land without rent to you
And may you die in Ireland.

May you never forget what is worth remembering
Or remember what is best forgotten
May you live as long as you wish
And have all you wish as long as you live
May the roof about us never fall in

And may we friends gathered below never fall out.

Saint Patrick was a gentleman

Who through strategy and stealth

Drove all the snakes from Ireland

Here's a toasting to his health

But not too many toastings

Lest you lose yourself and then

Forget the good Saint Patrick

And see those snakes again.

The lyrical quality of the toasts is obvious. There is a pattern and rhyme to them which remains within the folk group. Note also that the culture of Ireland, as in the belief in long leases and low rents, is so ingrained that it is placed into a toast. So, too, the popular legends as in St. Patrick and the snakes are toasted but used as a warning for too much drink. The Irish are aware that the recognition of their love of drinking is widespread, but these toasts delightfully celebrate and acknowledge it. There's an insouciance inherent in the toasts which make them appealing as they often cross ethnic lines and are adopted by others.

Finally, Irish St. Louisans, as well as all Irish, exclaim at the end of each toast, Slainte!, which is pronounced "slawn-cheh." Its simple meaning is "your health," the generous greeting of all toasts.

Irish Superstitions: Beyond the Four-Leaf Clover

Although most St. Louis Irish informants deny that they are superstitious, the evidence is not there. They are not alone in their disavowal of those "old wives' tales." Most people deny the belief!! But for a culture famous for the legends of the fairies, bashees, and the little people, their denial is not very convincing. Actually, all of us recognized that there are "gods" "out there" and continue to develop our own ways to bow to them. We say we recognize their power, but we want to try our own magic transference. As the commercial says: "It's not weird if it works."

Again these folk beliefs revolve around the rites of passage in the Irish culture.

LUCK

The shamrock, sometimes called a four-leaf clover, is the most common and popular good luck charm for all Irishmen. It is believed that if you possess a four-leaf clover, especially if you found it yourself, you will have good luck for the rest of your life and will be immune to the spells of the fairies, banshees, and witches. However, an Irishman must keep the good luck clover hidden and never give it to anyone. This will surely break the luck. Aside: some Irish tombstones have a four-leaf clover engraved on them so that the deceased may have an easier time getting to heaven. (Of course, not only Irish believe in the four-leaf clover. It has passed through many cultures.)

Always plant potatoes on Good Friday.

Never ever "cut" Irish whiskey with anything. It must be taken straight. If you mix it with anything you will definitely have bad luck.

If when you stand up, your chair falls over, you will have bad luck before the day is over.

While eating supper, do not turn off any lights or one of the people eating at the table will not be around for the next year's meal.

A red-haired woman will give you bad luck if you accidentally bump into one of them.

If a rabbit crosses your path as you are driving or walking you will have bad luck before the day is over. But, if you are carrying a rabbit's foot, you can cancel the bad luck. This is an example of a conversion superstition where one can counteract the supposed bad luck.

The mother of the first girl in the family to marry must give her daughter her gold wedding band to ensure good luck and abundance for the rest of her married life. If the mother does this for the first daughter to marry, it is believed that all the girls in the family will have the same luck transferred to them when they marry.

Never call out a person's name three times as it will bring bad luck to the caller and to the person called.

A cricket found in the house must never be killed as it will bring good luck to the house.

Always cut your hair during a full moon to guarantee good luck forever.

Never accept a lock of hair from your lover; it will cause bad luck.

A crowing hen is very bad luck. If it comes into your home, someone will die within the year.

FOLK MEDICINE

If you want to cure rheumatism, wear an iron ring on the ring finger of your left hand.

To cure a sore throat, use a poultice of hot potatoes tied around the neck.

To cure stomach pains or stomach disease tie mint leaves around your stomach.

To heal stitches after surgery, rub the stitches with unsalted butter. It must be unsalted!

Rub a peeled potato on warts to remove them. But don't forget to bury the potato after rubbing the wart.

If you have a disease, any disease, go to a wake and let the hand of the corpse touch you. (This was very popular in Ireland as many informants related, but practiced little here.)

Washing your face with the dew from a May morning will rid the face of freckles.

Carrot juice, boiled, must be drunk as hot as possible to cure infections.

HOLIDAYS

Never do laundry on New Year's Day; you will be washing out good luck from your clothes.

Sweep the dirt of the floor out the front door at the stroke of midnight on New Year's Eve to rid the house of bad luck.

Always eat herring on Christmas Day to ensure good luck for the next year.

On each of the 12 days of Christmas, eat a mince pie to ward off any disease. (Mince pies were believed to be made up of the gifts of the Magi to the Christ Child.)

If Christmas Day is on a Monday, it will mean good luck for everyone.

CHILDREN

If a boy baby is born after his father dies, it is believed that he can cure illnesses with his hands.

Attach a piece of iron to a newborn's clothing until he is baptized for protection.

The Changeling is a very popular legend in Irish lore. When a fairy has a baby, it is often a "deformed creature," as the stories go. So the fairies try to steal a healthy baby from an Irish home and replace it with her "changeling." Irish women, especially new mothers, fear these changelings deeply. To prevent the fairies from trading babies, a crucifix is sometimes placed under the crib. Sometimes iron tongs are placed on the bed. Other times, the clothing of the father of the child is draped over the baby. Almost all St. Louis informants knew of the changeling stories, did not practice it they said, but many still used the crucifix under the crib.

Eating oatmeal right after giving birth can prevent fairies from bringing changelings to the crib. Also putting unsalted butter on the baby's mouth will keep changelings away. (Note the use of unsalted butter. It is very common in Irish folk beliefs and the reasons are not clear.)

Babies born at midnight or close to midnight have the power to control ghosts and fairies.

Never take an unbaptized baby from his home. If it must be done, sprinkle the baby with holy water and make the sign of the cross on the forehead of the child.

When an Irish woman wishes to have a child she should first check all the handkerchiefs in the house. If there is a knot in any of them, she will never get pregnant until she undoes it. (Some Irish men informants have their own opinion on this belief! Some tell me they tie the knots themselves.)

The first lock of hair and the first trimmings from the fingernails of the baby should be wrapped in linen and placed under the crib or bed. The child will never have convulsions if it is done.

Take a newborn to a "holy well" and bless him to protect him from illness. (Informants spoke about "holy wells" in Ireland which were like spring water. Washing or even drinking the water from these wells was a very popular tradition as it was believed that the water had magical effects. The holy water from a Catholic Church, they relayed, has the same effect and is used in every home.)

MISCELLANEOUS FOLK BELIEFS

If a person stumbles at a grave site, it means bad luck will visit him. If he falls when he stumbles at the grave site, he will die within the year.

Never salute anyone with your left hand. Not only will it give both of you bad luck, but it will sever a friendship.

Rub a candle that was used at a wake over a burn to cure it.

If a person's ear itches, a friend in purgatory is asking for his prayers.

Never do anything important on a Friday. Nothing good will follow.

Never wash your hands at the same time as someone else in the same basin. Bad luck all around.

Destroy all eggshells after eating the egg. Fairies like to live in eggshells.

Never place shoes on a table or chair. It is an omen of something bad.

A horseshoe nailed above the door will bring good luck when hung as if a "U." If the horseshoe was a gift, never hang it anywhere; bad luck will follow. But if a person finds his own horseshoe that will guarantee good luck when hung above the door as the letter "U" so the luck won't run out.

Many of the folk beliefs that St. Louis Irish informants provided for research are clearly popular "American" superstitions. With some variations, it appears assimilation has taken place but it may be a double force. The Irish in St. Louis wanted to define themselves as American and as English-speaking they were more easily integrated. As mentioned earlier, it was initially difficult to collect Irish-St. Louis lore. The actual examples, however, are very similar to American folkways. One conclusion is obvious: the Irish in St. Louis, coming here in large numbers and very early in the city's history, transmitted their lore, tempered by the St. Louis experience, and St. Louisans accepted the pattern. The lore of the Irish became one with the lore of the city. Arguably, no other ethnic group can be tied so closely to the culture of the city as the Irish can.

The argument is even stronger when Halloween is considered. Under the heading of superstitions in folklore research, no holiday highlights these practices more than Halloween. Black cats, witches, ghosts, zombies, ghouls, and other strange creatures are all inherently fearful. Legend tells us that they love to appear on October 31, as some say, to celebrate the dead.

To those who wear costumes, dressed like these monsters, trick or treating for some reward is their primary, customary "job." People of all ages in St. Louis go door-to-door disguised as something or someone else, ask the owner an oft-repeated joke, which he pretends to have never heard and the goblin gets a treat. This ritual custom has long been identified with St. Louis. National media have recognized it. Where did it start?

With anonymity being part of the definition of folklore, a definite answer is not known. But in Ireland, for centuries people would dress in costumes and go from door to door to get something for the legendary Muck Olla who was wandering the neighborhoods that night looking for food or money. The costumed reveler would have to "perform" in order to be rewarded with something for the mythical Muck Olla. One argument is that this Irish custom is the origin of trick or treating in America. The addition of telling a joke or story, the argument continues, came from the Irish who settled in St. Louis.

Add the element of the ill-defined boundaries of Kerry Patch where many Irish originally settled. The area was constantly shifting and moving westward in St. Louis, and the Halloween tradition grew and moved with it. Was this the "unlearned" learning element of the Irish assimilating with their folkways?

Remember the movie *Meet Me in St. Louis?* In the Halloween scene where Tootie, played by Margaret O'Brien, was looking for her Halloween trick or treats, she carried flour with her. In Ireland, it was believed that you could capture or control a fairy or leprechaun on Halloween by throwing flour on them. In effect you would "kill them." This would prevent these harmful pests from snatching more people to take back with them to their unknown homes, which some believed was hell.

Tootie and her friends followed the tradition of the flour by going to the homes of their "enemies" or so they thought. Of course, the prank backfired, but eventually all worked out well Hollywood style. By the way, interestingly, Grandpa advised Tootie to make the flour wet so it would really stick on the "enemy." Clearly, Grandpa is an excellent example of how folklore is transmitted. He is the patriarch making certain that Tootie follows the ritual he practiced as a youngster. Tootie responds to the classic transmission of lore!

Don't forget that the St. Louis streets in the movie were filled with bonfires during the Halloween scene. The fires are concrete residuals from the days of Celtic lore. At Samhain, legends tell us that witches or animals were burned or that fires were lit to welcome the dead back to life or that bonfires were started to recreate the warm, welcoming Sun. St. Louis in 1904, as portrayed in the movie, kept the traditions alive!

LEPRECHAUNS AND THEIR "FRIENDS"

All students of folklore become acquainted, on various levels, with the "fairies" of Irish lore. The term often encompasses all the legends surrounding leprechauns, changelings, the banshee, the Pooka, the Dullahan and other various mysterious characters. The stories are legion in Ireland itself and, certainly, made their way to countries where the Irish immigrated.

St. Louis informants spoke little or nothing about these characters. They acknowledged that they had heard of them but had not experienced them here. But the legends still persist for some of the "fairy" groups. A brief word is necessary.

The banshee legends have been circulating for years in the St. Louis area. Famous for their piercing scream, the banshee is always a woman in St. Louis stories. She can be dressed as an old hag or a washer woman who appears to be washing blood from clothes. In one story she is riding a black horse. But in all the stories when she appears and wails her signature scream, there is no mistaking what it is: the banshee! For her scream, usually heard at night, portends death for someone. That someone? The legend further explains that the banshee can only cry for five Irish families: O'Briens, O'Connors, O'Gradys, Kavanaughs, and O'Neills. St. Louis legends add another family name starting with "Mc."

In the St. Louis area people have claimed to hear the distinctive mourning wail in Babler State Park, Rockwoods Reservation, and near Zombie Road in Wildwood. She has been seen riding on a horse, wailing, along the Meramec River in Valley Park, and on the same horse across the river on Poag Road near Edwardsville, Illinois. These supernatural legends, often urban belief tales (see Chapter 2) add a measure of a total Irish lore to the area.

Leprechauns are probably the most famous of the "fairies" in Irish lore. Legends tell us there were shoemakers, tiny in stature, usually drunk (not so much to be mentally deficient!), and self-proclaimed guardians of the pots of gold which the invaders to Ireland left behind. The folk are taught that if anyone catches the leprechauns, he will get the pot of gold, but the little folk are very clever and carry magical coins with them. They promise gold coins to the captured to bribe him. When they leave the coin will turn to sawdust or disappear. The leprechaun himself can vanish quickly and must be watched very carefully.

There are hundreds of legends about the "wee folk" which describe them in various roles, almost all mischievous. Many Irish people know of their constant presence without admitting it, of course. But for students of folklore, their antics represent an interesting and entertaining collection of legends.

The most feared of all the fairies in Ireland is the Pooka. It always roams the countryside after dark and can assume many forms. The most common form for the Pooka is that of a wild horse with a long, flowing mane who runs all over the countryside tearing up property and crops. In many legends the Pooka can speak and call for people to ride with him on his nightly runs. If the person refuses to come out of his home, the Pooka will, undoubtedly, destroy his property. Some say that if a person throws a gift to the Pooka he will be saved.

Many informants knew of the Pooka from folktales but not one person recounted any of the tales in St. Louis. It is interesting to note that on the popular drama series, *Boardwalk Empire*, on HBO, the Irish immigrants who are central to the storyline, discuss the Pooka as the cause of the tragedies befalling the families.

One other of the fairy people popular in Irish lore is the Dullahan, better known as the headless horseman. Washington Irving, in his *Legend of Sleepy Hollow*, made the Dullahan a part of American literary folklore. The classic Dullahan rides a black horse and carries his head in the crook of his arm. He rides his horse at any time of the day, as different from the other fairies, and nothing can stop him. Gates, for instance, open when they hear the galloping horse. But if the Dullahan catches anyone watching him ride, legend tells us that he will throw blood on the person and curse him to die. If, however, the person has something made of gold, the Dullahan will not bother him as the headless horseman fears gold. Lastly, some Irish legends have the Dullahan calling out someone's name, which is a persistent theme in fairy lore, and that person will die immediately.

Again, St. Louis informants knew of the Dullahan from Irish lore but never heard talk of it. Some appeared so fearful that they avoided mentioning the name for fear of consequences.

One person, however, mentioned that he heard that a popular video game featured the headless horseman. So he concluded that this fairy is no longer a threat!

Without question, all the fairy legends from Ireland and their dissemination in America have contributed to our fascination with ghostly lore. American supernatural legends, sometimes morphing into urban belief tales, are very popular. Stories in St. Louis locations about zombies, ghosts, specter hitchhikers, walking corpses, hooked men, and even banshees have been told for decades and are still being recited (see Chapter 2). Again, the Irish may not admit this contribution to our culture, or even be aware of it, but storytellers continue to tell them.

Paddy and Mick or Seamus and Mike?

You want a friend? Find an Irishman. You crave a good story? Find an Irishman. Want to hear a good joke? Find an Irishman. Perhaps no culture has a more positive stereotype than the Irish: friendly, caring, never strangers, good-hearted, generous, and good companions. Their blessings and toasts reflect these qualities. Their jokes reinforce the attributes, primarily with the humor of self-effacement. They take life seriously, but never themselves. Informants may have needed persuasion to talk about some aspects of their lore, but they were never reluctant with a joke.

WHAT IS IRISH DIPLOMACY?

It's the ability to tell a man to go to hell so that he will look forward to making the trip.

HAVE YOU HEARD ABOUT THE IRISH BOOMERANG?

It never comes back; it just sings songs about how much it wants to go back to Ireland.

Two Irishmen were out shooting ducks. One hit a duck on his first shot. The duck landed right at the foot of the companion. "You should have saved the bullet," he shouted. "The fall would have killed him anyway."

Seamus was asked if he understood Italian. "I do if it's spoken in Irish."

The young son: "Mom, there's a stranger at our door."

Mother: "Does he have a bill?"

Son: No, just a regular nose."

WHY ARE IRISH JOKES SO SIMPLE?

So Englishmen can understand them.

Doctor: "Well, Paddy. I can't quite diagnose your problem. It must be the drink."

How do you define an Irish husband?

A man who hasn't kissed his wife in ten years but will kill the man who does.

Paddy: "That's all right doc. I know how you feel. I'll come back tomorrow when you're sober.'

WHY DO IRISH THINK THAT JESUS WAS IRISH?

Because he was 33, lived at home, thought his mother was a virgin, and she thought he was God.

WHY DOES IT TAKE FIVE IRISHMEN TO CHANGE A LIGHTBULB?

One to change the bulb and four to discuss how grand the bulb was.

Father O'Connor walked into church and saw a man sitting on the altar.

"What do you want, young man?" he asked him.

"I am God,' said the man.

Father O'Connor rushed to the rectory and called Bishop O'Gorman.

"Bishop, there's a man in St. James who says he's God. What do I do?"

"Take no chances," says the bishop,
"look busy."

WHAT DO AN IRISH CATHOLIC PRIEST AND A PINT OF GUINNESS HAVE IN COMMON?

A black body, a white collar, and if you get a bad one, it'll tear the ass off you!

Maureen and Seamus have been married for a long time. One night Maureen says to Seamus, "I know you have slept with many lasses before me. I won't be mad, but will you tell me how many?"

What do you call an Irishman who knows how to control his wife?

A bachelor

"Maureen, my little shamrock, you should know that I have never slept with any other woman except you. I was awake with all of them."

Mike lay in a hospital covered with bandages and only slits for the eyes. Paddy comes to visit. "What happened to you, Mike?" Mike says, "I came out of the pub and a car raced down the street and knocked me through the plate glass of the pub." "Oh, God be blessed," says Paddy, "it's a good thing you were wearing those bandages or you'd be cut to ribbons."

The two basic lessons to teach the Irish jig: 1. Serve alcohol; 2. Lock the bathroom door.

Seamus was reading the paper and saw in the obits that he had died. Startled, he called Murph and told him he had died. Murphy says, "Where are you calling from?"

Mrs. Murphy: "Why don't you give up drinking, smoking, and carousing?"

Seamus: "It's too late for that."

Mrs. Murphy: "It's never too late!"

Seamus: "Well, there's no rush then."

Eileen followed her husband to the pub. She saw him

ordering a pint of Guinness. "How can you come here and drink that awful stuff?" Says Mike, "See and you thought I was enjoying myself."

WHAT'S LITTLE AND GREEN AND STICKS TO YOUR BUMPER?
A leprechaun who didn't look both ways.

O'Leary's wife died in an accident. The police asked him if she said anything before she died. O'Leary: "She spoke without interruption for forty years."

WHERE DOES AN IRISH FAMILY GO ON VACATION?
To a different pub.

HOW CAN YOU TELL YOU'RE BEING FOLLOWED BY A LEPRECHAUN?
Those tiny green hairs on your toilet seat!

WHAT'S THE DIFFERENCE BETWEEN AN IRISH WEDDING AND AN IRISH FUNERAL?
One less drunk.

Murph called for an ambulance. "Hurry, my wife is about to have a baby." "Is this her first baby?" "No, you idiot, this is her husband."

Dogtown: Irish Essence in St. Louis

Dogtown, a neighborhood in the southwest part of the city of St. Louis, is the epicenter of all things Irish, or things that want to be Irish, or history that pretends to be Irish, or of residents who are intensely proud of their Irish inheritance and are determined to keep it pure.

Although there is an "official" St. Patrick's Parade in downtown St. Louis, the "real official authentic green 'craic' parade" takes place every St. Patrick's Day in Dogtown. Thousands, perhaps "millions"—as some locals claim—come in their finest green clothes, inscribed with "Irish" invitations to kiss; bedecked in graffiti buttons proclaiming leprechauns as relatives; waving buckthorn shillelaghs; swirling green beer; and walking for hours through the neighborhood. The parade has become so popular its contagion has spread throughout the St. Louis area. It's equivalent to an official holiday in the city! And if you're not Irish on any other day, you are on March 17. Those who make it home that evening carry with them the smell of corned beef and cabbage. The celebration is so important and vital to the Irish culture that the Catholic Church allows eating meat if March 17 happens to fall on a Friday during Lent! No more important stamp of approval is needed! Dogtown is the "olde sod."

Given all this shamrock tossing and Irish flag waving, ironically, most of the residents of blue-collar Dogtown know very little about actual Irish culture. Visit Seamus McDaniel's or Pat's Bar and Grill and no one will be discussing James Joyce or Michael Collins or the Dublin economy. Beer and baseball, the neighborhood activities, and the parish church are more frequent topics for conversation. But Bob and John Corbett have no problem with this paradox. They believe that the residents of Dogtown may not know much about Irish culture, but they definitely practice the Irish lifestyle.

That lifestyle, according to Bob Corbett, consists of three values: family, community, and religion, meaning Catholicism. Corbett believes that these three principles have always governed the communities of Ireland and became the foundation of Dogtowners. But how did this become established as Irish?

In his blog for the Dogtown neighborhood, based on his exhausting research, Corbett writes:

The Irish have never been the dominant ethnic group in Dogtown. I first discovered this when I catalogued the U.S. census for Dogtown. The largest ethnic group in Dogtown were German, followed by Irish, then Italian, and even a significant number of Croatians. But the neighborhood was Irish in "spirit." Most of the ethnic groups were Roman Catholic. Virtually all of these people were working class with little education. They came mostly after 1860 when the diocese of St. Louis opened a mission in that year at St. James. The first church burned and a second was built along with an elementary school. It is important to note that from 1860 until 1952, EVERY Pastor at St. James was born in Ireland, ordained in Ireland, served as an assistant pastor in Ireland, and came to St. Louis as a missionary priest. The pastor was one of the very few people in the area who was educated and who had the most contact with the neighborhood. For guidance and service, not just religion, people talked to the priest and he taught them a life centered on Irish Catholicism. The Germans, French, Italians, and Croatians, among others learned Irish culture as a way to be and a way to imitate, having no idea they were living Irish culture.

(It should be noted that the role of religion cannot be overstated for the Irish. Many of the informants spoke, with reverence, of the traditions of their parish which became not only private devotions, but also bonding agents for the community. For example, many recounted the religious calendar: During Advent, the weeks before Christmas, most attended daily Mass to prepare for the coming of the Christ child. Then it was Mass at midnight on Christmas Eve which was followed by a celebration of food into the early morning hours.

During Lent, the six weeks before Easter, daily Mass was again the accepted practice. Irish parishioners gave up candy, cigarettes, gum, and even beer (!), as personal penitence. During Lent there was usually a service on Wednesday nights with the recitation of the rosary and benediction. Friday nights during Lent, the Stations of the Cross were recited, sometimes involving a procession. On Holy Thursday night, St. Louis Irish (and others led by the Irish tradition) would "make the seven churches" to spend time with Christ in the Blessed Sacrament on the day before His death. Some Irish believe it is important to walk to the churches as a final penance for Lent.

Other devotions took place as rituals which continue to bind the community. There were First Fridays to the Sacred Heart; Tuesday night devotions to Our Lady of Perpetual Help; novenas—nine consecutive days of prayer and devotion in the parish; even a two-week mission is held in a parish but attended by many other parishes and parishioners.

But prayer was not the only tradition that bound the community. Churches had a Holy Name Society, a Legion of Mary, a scapular society, a rosary society, a St. Vincent de Paul group, among many others.

In all these services and societies the parish priest played the most vital role. He was a constant presence throughout the neighborhood available to all. The black cassock became a folk costume immediately identified by all.

Thus the melting pot of Dogtown immigrants became a center for Irish "culture," and retains that definition even today. For

Dogtowners like the Corbett family, it is essential to maintain the "Irish way of life" for the future of the community.

It is this paradox in the depth of "Irish" culture in Dogtown and St. Louis in general that is ideal research for the folklorist. As mentioned earlier, Irish informants were reluctant to identify specific folk genres from their culture. Their assimilation to "America" was more important. But, as noted, the Irish lore is there, primarily in the overriding *spirit* of the culture and then in their delightful folk texts.

DOGTOWN: NAMED FOR DOGS?

Nowhere is the folklore of the Irish more realized than in the origin of the name of the "Irish Hill," Dogtown. The various stories of the origin of the name satisfy a criterion of folklore to have different versions for a folk text. Traditionally transmitted, over generations, are two more, and finally some basis of a "truth." Dogtown's name has all of them.

There are at least nine versions of how "Dogtown" got its name. And there are as many groups of residents who believe one or more of them to be factual. Judge for yourselves which are cogent:

1. The Irish loved dogs and kept many of them as pets in the neighborhood. They allowed them to roam and become part of everyone's household.
2. The immigrant mine and clay workers who came to the area kept dogs as protection for their families while they were at work.
3. Homeless people were evicted from Forest Park in the 1876 to make room for park construction. They built shacks, called "dog houses," in the area which is very near to Forest Park, and were slandered as "those poor dogs."

4. During the 1904 World's Fair, held in Forest Park, very near to the area of Dogtown, the Philippine exhibit was one of many world entries. It was the largest at the Fair and was manned by Filipino tribes known as Igorots. There were a total of seven tribes numbering more than a thousand natives. And their favorite food was dog! The city of St. Louis, with help from then Secretary of War William Howard Taft, supplied the Igorots with twenty dogs a day for their meals. Legend tells us that the dogs were roasted daily in plain view of interested visitors to the Fair. Further, the legend states that the dogs were gathered from the area near the fairgrounds which came to be called Dogtown.

5. Dogs were a constant nuisance to the horses of the merchants who drove their wagons through the area. In disgust they called the area Dogtown.

6. St. James is known for their championship soccer teams. They needed a name to differentiate them from other Catholic league teams. Dogtown St. James was the choice.

7. Many Irish worked on the St. Louis riverfront and they called their boats "doggeries." Moving to the area of Dogtown was a natural naming rite for them.

8. Irish immigrants, by Americans, were called shanty Irish, lace curtain Irish, and dog Irish. The name was given to the area where they settled.

But recently, Bob Corbett and his fellow historians, believe they have discovered the definitive reason for the name Dogtown:

9. The original settlers were coal miners. They started by digging small holes and literally dug the coal out of the ground with their shovels. The surface resembled an area of small holes like those which dogs would dig. Looking in a dictionary of mining terms, the name "doghole" is

used to define the small opening in a coal mine, similar to those dug by the early miners in St. Louis. The "doghouse" was the small house where the miners would change their clothes. Furthermore, "dogtown" is a common term for shelters surrounding a mineral deposit.

The historical weight in this last definition gives the most credence to the nickname for the area. All the facts are there. But the folk have their own facts—at least nine of them! The origin of the name of Dogtown will continue to be part of the folk tradition, accurate, romantic, or just plain wrong . . . it's still the lore of the folk.

The Irish have given roots to the culture of St. Louis. One day a year it is happily very obvious. But the other days of the year, it is "under the radar" but just as significant as March 17. The types of lore—sayings, folk beliefs, blessings, jokes, vocabulary, grammar, rituals, and others—are all here, and recognized. The spirit of each text, however, is the important contribution of the Irish: the sense of fun, friendship, family, mystery, reverence, community, a higher reality, and living, laughing, loving life to leave a legacy.

Let Bob Corbett sum it up. This is his favorite Irish saying for a wedding proposal: Would you like to be buried with my people?

No words are necessary. Slainte!

CHAPTER 10

Bosnians in St. Louis

There are the "scrubby Dutch," the Italians from The Hill, the Irish, Slavic, Greek, Jewish, African-Americans, Polish, and numerous ethnicities who have contributed to the folklore of the St. Louis region. (Many of them were discussed in my previous book *Passing It On*.) To this proverbial melting pot of lore and aiding the definition of St. Louis as a "gateway" welcoming city, add the rich culture of the Bosnians.

The settlement of Bosnians in the St. Louis region is a significant and inspiring story that echoes many chapters of immigration throughout American history. Now, numbering more than 70,000 in the St. Louis area, most Bosnians came because of the Serbian program of "ethnic cleansing" in their native Bosnia-Herzegovina. The war, from 1992 to 1995, destroyed much of the historic and naturally beautiful country. Genocide was the worst since World War II. Mass graves are being found almost twenty years later. The rich history of the country dates as far back as the Ottoman Empire. Universal recognition of Bosnian culture and contribution came as recently as the Winter Olympic Games in their capital of Sarajevo in 1984. Then the war followed. More than 100,000 Bosnians were killed and more than two million were displaced to all parts of the world. The physical and emotional destruction of Bosnia and its people defies description. But their spirit and culture did not die.

The United States allowed Bosnians a haven as refugees. Because of the availability of jobs, the low cost of living, affordable housing, and members of the community already here, St. Louis was *the* destination. The area in South St. Louis around Bevo Mill was the center of Bosnian migration. Because of their industry, the neighborhood has developed into a destination site. Restaurants, bakeries, grocery stores, taverns, bookstores, even a Bosnian Chamber of Commerce have been established. Today there are more Bosnians in St. Louis than any other place outside of Bosnia itself. Secondary migration from other parts of the United States continues to increase the St. Louis Bosnian population. Based on a strong work ethic, a desire for citizenship and roots, and a strong religious tradition, their contributions to the culture of St. Louis are growing significantly.

Basic and vital to their contribution to St. Louis are the indestructible oral traditions of the Bosnians. To a St. Louis folklore long established and rich in meaning and reflection, the Bosnians, yearning for assimilation and acceptance, have added another important layer. On the surface some interpretations of their lore are apparent. Collectively, seeing many variations of the same folk type, can offer a definition of the Bosnian cultural character. Some examples of their lore are, however, clearly stated. As in most regions of the country, there is a clear understanding of what it means to be from that region. In *Passing It On*, also, there were many examples from the folk on how a person knows he is from St. Louis. The examples are legion and are still being collected.

Perhaps, in an effort to be assimilated more easily, Bosnians, in a delightful self-deprecating way, give many examples of what it means to be a Bosnian and for St. Louisans "how" to recognize a Bosnian. As a function of folklore, no matter how crude the humor, this is an exercise in education where the anti-Bosnian faction is beaten at their own game. Here are many of the examples:

You Know You Are Bosnian When . . .

Your neighbor comes over every day for coffee, uninvited.

You have twelve consonants and two vowels in your surname.

You have "pita" for dinner at least four days a week. Pita is a Bosnian folk food staple. It is a pastry filled with ground meat, or cheese or even other fillings.

You eat a loaf of bread every day for lunch! Bread may be the most identifiable food for Bosnians. It is made every day in the traditional Bosnian home and at Bosnian bakeries it is a bestselling item to non-Bosnian St. Louisans. Even the St. Louis chain grocery stores make Bosnian bread for all customers, Bosnian or not. *Kruh,* as in several other St. Louis ethnic groups, has become a symbol of acceptance.

You chop up onions and *then* decide what to have for dinner.

You tuck your undershirt into your underwear.

Your mother bakes a cake without oil, sugar, flour, or eggs and calls it a "war cake."

Your time is divided "before" and "after" the war.

Your father wears only striped pajamas to bed.

Your morning begins with some strong Turkish coffee and a cigarette.

Your home has a manual coffee grinder.

You have *sarma* for dinner three nights a week. Pita the other days! Sarma is a traditional meal made of cabbage leafs stuffed with ground meat and rice.

Your home has fine lace doilies (*heklanje*) on every piece of furniture, including the television.

You begin most sentences with *svega mi.* (I swear on it!)

Zimnica is made every September. This is canning vegetables for the winter meals.

Proverbs, sayings, stories, legends, jokes, rituals, folk foods, folk music, and other folk texts from the Bosnian culture have melded well with St. Louis lore. Significantly, Bosnian lore is an important example of the oral tradition surviving when other symbols have been destroyed. Add their lore to that being "passed" around in St. Louis for decades and a new, fortunate tradition is established.

The following examples of Bosnian folklore were collected from St. Louis informants, all of whom are Bosnian. The list is certainly not meant to be exhaustive. Researching Bosnian folklore in St. Louis is a new undertaking. The perspective of time is necessary to understand and interpret how the lore mirrors the St. Louis experience of the new Bosnian culture. What is presented is a taste of the folk materials still in the community that needs documentation and preservation.

Bosnian Proverbs

For decades, proverbs have served a basic function of folklore: education. From the erudition of someone like Ben Franklin to the "unlearned-learned" tradition of the common man in America, the metaphor of a proverb is teaching something. The same is true of the proverbs or aphorisms of other cultures. Bosnians settling in St. Louis have brought their sayings with them.

Tko drugome jamu kopa sam u nju pada.
If you dig a trap for someone else, you will fall in it yourself.

Tko rano, rani, dvije srece grabi.
If you get up early, you are lucky more than once. (The early
bird catches the worm?)

Nema vatre bex dima.
There is no smoke without fire. The same identical caution:
Where there's smoke there's fire.

Bolje vrabac u ruci, nego golum no grani.
A chickadee is the hand in better than a pigeon on a branch.
(A bird in the hand is worth two in the bush.)

Gdje ti mnogo obecavaju, malu torbu ponesi.
When people are promising a lot to you, bring a small bag.
(This could be a variant of: don't believe everything you
hear; or be careful of smooth-talking salesmen.)

Osoba koja laze za tebe isto tako ce lagati i protiv tebe.
A person who lies for you will also lie against you.

Gvozde se juje dok je vruce.
Iron is best worked when it's hot. (St. Louis version: Strike
while the iron's hot. Both are advising not to waste time in a
venture which is probably a good risk.)

Lijepe rijeci nece napuniti praznu serpu.
Beautiful words don't put porridge in the pot.

Ocisti svoju okucnicu, pa onda reci komsijama da ociste
njihove.
Clean your own yard before you ask others to clean theirs.

Nemojte biti obmanjeni suzama onog ko moli za nesto.
Don't be mislead by the tears of a beggar.

Onaj ko poslusa prvu zeninu rijec, slusat ce i sve druge rijeci kroz citav zivot.
A man who hears the first word of his wife must listen to the second forever.

Dvije stvari upravljaju svijetom: nagrada i kasna.
Two things rule the world: reward and punishment.

Oci prepisivaca ce uvijek biti pune suza.
The eyes of all cheats are full of tears.

Iver ne pada daleko od klade.
A piece of wood doesn't land far from the tree. (When we talk about generations and other likely scenarios: An apple doesn't fall far from the tree.)

Nije zlato sve sto sija.
Not all shiny things are golden. (The obvious popular caution: All that glitters is not gold.)

Pas koji laje ne ujeda.
The dog that barks doesn't bite. (The popular version: A barking dog never bites.)

Drvo ne raste naopacke.
A tree does not grow from the sky.

Budala ce da potrosi sve sto je neko tesko stekao kroz citav zivot.
A silly man wastes away in the middle of plenty.

Lav ne moze cuti viastito rikanje.
A lion cannot hear its own roar.

Tko s vragom tikve sadi, o glavu mu se obiju.
If one sows pumpkins with the devil, they will bash onto one's head (No clear corollary in American proverbs, but a suggested one, "If you play with pigs you'll get dirty.")

Not surprisingly, many of the Bosnian proverbs are very similar to those found in America and specifically in St. Louis. The reflection of their applicability is the interesting function. How do people use the sayings? Are they all used in the same way: Educational? Cautionary? Simple communication? Will the Bosnian versions of the same saying morph into the American vernacular? Do both genders use them? Although the circumstances where these basic orally transmitted folk texts are unknown, significantly, the similarities to American versions are already there as another basis for assimilation.

Superstitions, Folk Beliefs, and Rituals

Americans are a superstitious people. Despite the negative connotation, this is not a bad folk theme. In St. Louis, for example, there are many folk beliefs carrying bad luck, but the region has developed "conversion" folk beliefs that negate the bad luck. (Complete discussion is in *Passing It On*.) This form of optimism is crucial to an understanding of the regional lore. The ability to see rituals and understanding what "fear of the deity" means is a positive reflection on a ritualistic society. (*Superstitio* is Latin for "standing in fear of the deity.")

The refugees from Bosnia to St. Louis have brought many examples of their folk beliefs with them. They are a welcome addition to a folk form already used to define a region. Again, some of their beliefs are variants of St. Louis practices and make for an easier assimilation.

If a person walks over the legs of someone sitting on the floor, he must go back over the legs or the person sitting on the floor will stop growing or have another form of bad luck. This Bosnian belief is an example of conversion lore, so common to the St. Louis region. Converting the bad luck to a void is important for the person sitting. Not to have retraced one's steps would create bad luck.

Bosnians love to hold on to things for "*uspomene*," memories. To throw away something someone considers important or sentimental to a family is bad luck for the person who pitches it.

Young ladies who wear "*pape*" or knitted socks even in the warmest weather will always have an easy pregnancy.

Never go outside or to bed with wet hair. One must wait at least two hours to avoid getting very sick. Otherwise, your brain will get inflamed.

"*Rakija*" (whiskey) is the chicken soup of Bosnian culture. It will cure anything and everything.

Never clip your fingernails or toe nails at night. You will get sick within the week. Also, never clip your nails on a Tuesday, which will also cause sickness. If it's at night on a Tuesday when you clip your nails, someone close to you will die! (Why Tuesday is chosen is a mystery to Bosnians who still believe the ritual and caution.)

If you accidentally bump heads with someone, you must bump them again to rid either of you from harm. If you don't "re-bump" some say that your parents will die. (Another example of a conversion folk belief.)

Never walk backwards. Again, if you do your parents will die.

One must never eat in the bed in which one sleeps. This can leave crumbs and other dirt and will eventually cause "*ograjsat*." This is a form of mental instability ranging from minimal stress to full blown bipolar disorder.

Never say anything as a joke or an aside, it might come true and is known as a *"slutit."* If, in a conversation, your friends and you are joking about illnesses and you laughingly say that you'll probably die of a brain tumor, for instance, or some other horrible death, you will be warned to "take it back." You have just awakened your "inner voice," or *"slutit."* Eventually what you mentioned will come to pass. So it is imperative to recant as a conversion.

The act of itching is the theme for several superstitions: Right hand itching, money going out. Left hand itching, money coming in. If your eyebrows or chin itch, good fortune is coming your way.

The wind (*"vjetar"*) is to be feared all the time. It is always an "ill wind," because it brings illness to those in it. Many Bosnians remark that they close their windows in very hot weather or even while driving as the wind will give them bad luck or cause illness.

For a bad cold, soak your socks in vinegar and then wear them to bed.

Never expose your back to a cold wind or draft (*"promaha"*). You run the risk, if a female, of freezing your ovaries; if a male, freezing your kidneys.

Never sit on the corner of a table; you'll never get married.

When seeing a new baby for the first time, one must never say it is beautiful, because you don't want to run the risk of the baby growing up to be ugly.

Never stand under a door sill while talking. Bad luck will follow.

Talking about someone in a bad way will give either you or the person talked about the hiccups.

Many of the examples listed are representative of Bosnian beliefs. Some Bosnian informants scoffed at the folk texts, and they do not practice them, as they say, but all of them had heard of the superstitious beliefs and know many people who use them and teach them religiously. You will notice, again, that many of them have related beliefs in the American culture. Origins of these beliefs along with many American ones are difficult to track. In fact anonymity is a hallmark of true folklore. Interestingly, the similarities in the beliefs will probably ease assimilation and add to the rich ethnicity of St. Louis.

Jokelore

The joke, sometimes identified as a riddle, is a universal folk text. Each society, culture, region, ethnicity has humor which reflects their beliefs or character. Often the jokes are about another culture or region, which also connotes a feeling or even opinion about the subject of the joke. Researchers have called this the "exoteric-esoteric" factor. It is acceptable for one group, for example, to tell jokes about themselves, but no other group can do it. And sometimes the jokes about a particular race or ethnic group might be esoteric and not understood by another. This form of joke helps create bonding, a basic function of folklore.

There has always been a series, often successive, of "slam" or exoteric jokes in American culture. Origins are speculative, but the chapters of immigration in American history have certainly contributed to their transmission. Polock, Dago, Kraut, Newfies, Aggies, and Blonde jokes, joined by the historical Little Audrey, Little Mary, and Little Janey have always depicted the subject as inferior, or dumb, or clueless. Add the classifications Moron, Idiot, Brillo, Redneck, Hoosier, or even Elephant Jokes, and the "other" culture, different from *the* American way, is clearly depicted.

Jokes from the Bosnian culture follow a similar clear pattern. Known as the people with the best sense of humor in the former Yugoslavia, telling jokes is a favorite form of communication, education, and bonding among Bosnians. Having suffered through the horrible atrocities of the nineties and being uprooted in a massive diaspora, it would seem that their sense of humor would be gone. The opposite is true. Bosnian informants told of telling jokes during the war, while in Bosnia, to keep sanity, and passing on these jokes to their children in their new homeland. This latter function of joking is an effort to keep the culture alive and making certain that they never forget what happened to them in Bosnia. They can laugh and joke about everything, including themselves. But who or what are the staples of their jokes? The archetypical characters, Mujo, Haso, Suljo, and Fata, the female of the quartet. As stock characters they would appear to be ignorant, but in truth, as the jokes often relate, they are aware, intelligent, clever, and truly funny characters.

(Interestingly, Bosnians also tell the "exoteric" joke. They like to joke about Ivica and Perica, said to be Croatian. These are Croatian stereotypes to Bosnians and are fair game to be joked about for their dumb acts. Here, again, Bosnians can joke about themselves, but as with other cultures, they can also joke about neighbors. Given the history of Yugoslavia, these jokes about Croatians certainly have some reflective purpose and no doubt serve as a release for Bosnians.)

An excellent example of the use of humor by Bosnians in the midst of a horrific war is the following:

Mujo and Sujo are walking along a country road during the war. Both of them had plenty of shlivovitz (plum brandy; the national liquor). They are almost home when Mujo notices a human head on the side of the road.

He screams, "Hey, Sujo, there's someone's head. Sujo, replied, "Are you sure?" "Yes," said Mujo, "it looks like our neighbor,

> Nermin . . . oh, no, it is Nermin." He picks up the head and says, "See it is our poor neighbor, Nermin." Sujo says with much aggravation, "It can't be. Nermin was much taller."

There is, of course, in this joke an element of the sick joke, so popular in the sixties and seventies in America. But there is also a note of resignation about the tribulations of the war. The joke seems to say that everyone knows that they can do nothing about the war. They don't accept it as something inevitable, but they know they are powerless. Humor, however, sick as it might be becomes a defense. It's a way to ward off the horrors of war hitting them. Perhaps it's an example of "slutit."

Here's a simple, funny, smart, and popular joke. Many countries are used instead of France, but the message is always the same.

A man from Bosnia and a man from France were talking about the important things in life. The man from France said: "For me, France is first, then my job, and then my family." The man from Bosnia said, "For me it is the opposite: first comes my family, then my job, and then France."

Milosevic* is convicted as a war criminal by the court. The judge does not know what would be the worst punishment to give him. A Bosnian suggests that he sentence Milosovic to live on a Bosnian pension.

Another example:

> Fata is not feeling well. So Mujo takes her to the hospital. After she is examined, the doctor comes out and tells Mujo that Fata is not looking good. Mujo tells the doctor, "I know

---

*Milosevic was the leader of a Greater Serbia and perpetrated the "ethnic cleansing" of the Bosnians in the 1990s. His atrocities were the worst since Hitler's and he died during his trial. Even though he was recognized as the devil by most Bosnians and much of the world, note the use of the humor in the following joke. Making fun of a Bosnian pension, which is the "worst" punishment to give the war criminal is strongly indicative of the very positive sense of humor Bosnians have.

that but she's a good mother and a good cook and that is why she is my wife."

A joke on semantics is universal. This one adds the element of the universal battle of man vs. woman.

Here's another example of a simple yet funny and typical Bosnian joke:

Mujo and Haso went to a football (soccer) game. They decided to make a bet: when the chosen team makes a goal, the other will buy the beer for both of them. The game ended in a 0-0 tie. Mujo said to Haso: "Let's go to the basketball game!"

Finally, here's another stock character joke with a new element:

An American, a German, and a Bosnian were asked how long it would take them to save up to buy Mercedes.

The American said he could buy it in one month.

The German said it would only take him twenty days to buy Mercedes.

Haso said, "I have to call my wife, Fata. She handles all our finances and would know how long it would take us to buy Mercedes."

He calls Fata. After an hour, he calls back: "So, Fata, did you figure it out? How long would it take us to buy Mercedes?"

Fata said, "About six months."

"What?" says Haso. "Why so long?"

"Take it easy," Fata says. "It's not my fault. You know that Mercedes is a big company with many, many people in it. It's not that easy!"

Folk Foods

The dumb blonde enters Bosnian jokes. But Fata is the one who takes care of all the finances for the family. This importance given to the wife or mother is typical of a Bosnian family. Again, there is a problem with communications and Fata understands the Mercedes one way, different from Haso. She is not wrong but the joke continues her stereotype.

There are many examples of Bosnian humor where the Bosnians joke about their perceived stupidity and compare themselves to others from the former Yugoslavia who are lazy. These jokes reflect actual life in Bosnia during and after the war. Finding work was not easy; so many Bosnians went to other countries, particularly Germany, to find a job. The assessment of the German employer often revolves around a joke about Bosnians' qualifications. The Bosnian protagonist readily admits he might be unaware, but he is certainly not lazy. This self-deprecation or self-effacement humor is a hallmark of Bosnian lore and all the more remarkable given their recent history.

Another example of Bosnian lore represents the structure of the family. The preachments of MOM, in American culture, often called Momisms, are easily recognized. All of us have been told often to wear clean underwear always! (In the earlier *Passing It On*, there is a whole chapter devoted to these expressions.) In the Bosnian home the woman is the head of the household. All members recognize it. The whole culture recognizes it. What "momma says" must be heeded.

You'll get sick from drinking cold water.

You should never take a shower every day; it will dry your skin off.

You must eat something with a spoon at least once a week.

Samo cekaj dok ti se babo vrati kuci.
Wait till your dad comes home. (Is this common to all mothers?)

Ako te udarim crna ce te krv obliti.
If I hit you, black blood will cover you.

You must always wear a *potkosulja* (undershirt) no matter what the weather.

You are always hungry and must eat; don't say you're not hungry; you are!

You are told that she already had you and your two sisters when she was your age.

The prevailing Bosnian wisdom? Just Listen!

Perhaps the biggest impact of the Bosnian culture on St. Louis folklore is their folk food. To gooey butter cake, pork steaks, toasted ravioli, and the ice cream cone, Bosnians have added many dishes, and tweaked them for their St. Louis experience. Bosnian restaurants, for example, originally established to maintain a taste of the homeland, have become destination points for St. Louis diners. St. Louis–based supermarkets have recognized the impact of Bosnian food and are making Bosnian "dinners" in their delis and Bosnian bread in their bakeries. Whole sections of Bosnian staples are also stocked in the aisles.

Although some Bosnian chefs, bakers, cooks, or restaurant owners, in an effort to become mainstream, shyly declare that they are making American food, the delicious product cannot be denied. Their pride may be hidden, but the result of introducing their food to the St. Louis folk is a positive aspect of diversity. Melding the new dishes creates a new folk food for St. Louis making the culture of the city richer.

Perspective does not allow researchers' conclusive interpretations of how much Bosnian food has affected the culture of St. Louis. But a quick glance at the products widely made and widely purchased suggests that the foundation is already here. Consider some examples:

Kruh, Bosnian sliced bread; delicious with sweet creamy butter and served immediately on diner's tables before the meal

Lepinja (or *lepini,* or *lepinji*) bread for sandwiches

Suho meso, a smoked beef

Tulumba, the signature dessert cake of the Bosnian dining experience, arrives dripping with syrup

Sarma, cabbage stuffed with beef and rice, rolled and cooked in a tomato sauce

Trahana, a tomato-based soup filled with dumplings

Cevapi, link sausages, served on gigantic "frisbees" of lepini, rival the Big Mac

Cupavci, a sponge cake filled with custard and topped with coconut

Turkish coffee, the stronger the better, is used to socialize, not to wake a person up. It becomes a ritual of drinking and relaxing and is often enjoyed four times a day.

"Bosnian pita," a phyllo dough stuffed with "anything": potatoes, vegetables, meat

The importance of bread in Bosnian culture cannot be overstated. In many Slavic and Middle Eastern countries, bread is the symbol of belonging. It often represents human dignity and carried or even worn as a "bread helmut" during a demonstration for rights. Many Bosnians bake bread every day to keep the traditions and meaning alive. In fact a few Bosnian bakeries sell nothing but bread helping to underscore its importance to the culture.

One constant of Bosnian food, already identified with American, is large quantities. Bosnian hosts have a need to make sure no one feels hungry and often "push" food just as Bosnian mothers do in their homes. The thinking is: What do you mean, you're not hungry? This question comes after a large meal when more food is served!

The study of Bosnian folklore and its impact on St. Louis culture is just beginning. With the documentation of more texts and the preservation of oral traditions, a clearer perspective can be found. The evidence is clear, however. Bosnians, in their short years of settlement in St. Louis have made a significant, diverse difference. Their long history of adapting did not diminish their optimistic character. This is a good match to St. Louis as "gateway," welcoming all and celebrating their contribution to the social fabric. Incidentally, the symbol of the Bosnian nation is the fleur-de-lis! A perfect fit for St. Louis! Coincidence or synchronicity? No matter, the Bosnian roots have been planted.

CONCLUSION

St. Louis Folklore

What's left? As has been discussed, the dynamism of folklore affects kids, seniors, men versus women, our educational system, established and new ethnicities, old and new ghostly legends and urban belief tales, ever-changing vocabulary, computers, occupations like nurses and lawyers, and even societal folk groups like quilters. Each has an identity; each has a function; each seeks validation, integration, and a voice. And each has the human need to pass on their "unlearned" learned lore. The collection and documentation, as has been discussed, allows for a greater and important understanding of our culture and of ourselves.

But, the living and the lore and the profound cultural changes go on and on and on. There is an ongoing need for the "voice-in-the-wilderness" folk to compensate and bond. This is where some new lore intrudes. Given the restlessness of the culture in the past several years, and the grassroots movements striving to be heard with louder voices, and the polarities seemingly forming over basic opposites, the folk are speaking with a more confident voice. The pronouncements are still traditional and anonymous and exist in different versions, all criteria for folklore, but their tone is elevated to a bitterness that was missing in earlier folk texts. But another recent polarity of folk genres attempts to elevate the lore to a more sincere, conciliatory level.

This new "sincerity" smacks of "Mayberry" or "The Beav" to many people. But it is a direct response to the vitriol these folk see in the current folk themes. These informants are painting a word picture of white picket fences surrounding bungalows where

182

neighborhoods were safe and sacred and the family was the highest of values.

The contrast with the tone of superior sarcasm and cool dominance could not be starker. These two forms of current lore are begging for collection, validation, and documentation. Having been successful in developing an identifiable folk voice with all the new language, new texts, pushing former sacred boundaries to reflect our new society, the folk are eager to keep their brand of lore mainstream. They are determined to pass it on. But their reflective lore is being challenged.

COMPANY CHRISTMAS PARTY

COMPANY MEMO

FROM: Joan Smith, Human Resources Director

TO: All Employees

DATE: November 1, 2012

SUBJECT: Gala Christmas Party

I'm happy to inform you that the company Christmas party will take place on December 22nd, starting at noon in the private room at the Brew House. There will be a cash bar and plenty of drinks!

We'll have a small band playing traditional carols; feel free to sing along. And don't be surprised if our CEO, Dave Jones, shows up dressed as Santa Claus! A Christmas tree will be lit at 1:00 pm. Exchanges of gifts among employees can be done at that time; however, no gift should be over $10 to make the giving of gifts easy for everyone's pockets. This gathering is only for employees!

Mr. Jones will make a special announcement at that time!

Merry Christmas to you and your family.

Joan

COMPANY MEMO

FROM: Joan Smith, Human Resources Director

TO: All Employees

DATE: November 2, 2012

SUBJECT: Gala Christmas Party

In no way was yesterday's memo intended to exclude our Jewish employees. We recognize that Hanukkah is an important holiday, which often coincides with Christmas, though unfortunately not this year. However, from now on, we're calling it our "Holiday Party." The same policy applies to any other employees who are not Christians and to those still celebrating Reconciliation Day. There will be no Christmas tree and no Christmas carols will be sung. We will have other types of music for your enjoyment.

Happy now?

Happy Holidays to you and your family.

Joan

COMPANY MEMO

FROM: Joan Smith, Human Resources Director

TO: All Employees

DATE: November 3, 2012

SUBJECT: Holiday Party

Regarding the note I received from a member of Alcoholics Anonymous requesting a non-drinking table, you didn't sign your name. I'm happy to accommodate this request, but if I put a sign on a table that read, "'AA Only," you wouldn't be anonymous anymore. How am I supposed to handle this?

Somebody?

And sorry, but forget about the gift exchange. No gifts are allowed since the union members feel that $10.00 is too much money and the executives believe $10.00 is a little chintzy.

REMEMBER: NO GIFT EXCHANGE WILL BE ALLOWED.

COMPANY MEMO

To: All Employees

DATE: November 4, 2012

SUBJECT: Generic Holiday Party

What a diverse group we are! I had no idea that December 20th begins the Muslim holy month of Ramadan, which forbids eating and drinking during daylight hours. There goes the party! Seriously, we can appreciate how a luncheon at this time of year doesn't accommodate our Muslim employees' beliefs. Perhaps the Brew House can hold off on serving your meal until the evening. Will that work?

Meanwhile, I've arranged for members of Weight Watches to sit farthest from the dessert buffet, and pregnant ladies will get the tables closed to the restrooms. Gays are allowed to sit with each other. Lesbians do not have to sit with gay men. Each group will have their own table.

Yes, there will be flower arrangements for the gay men's table.

To the person asking permission to cross dress, the Brew House asks that no cross-dressing be allowed, apparently because of concerns about confusion in the restrooms. Sorry.

We will have booster seats for short people.

Low-fat food will be available for those on a diet.

I am sorry to report that we cannot control the amount of salt used in the food. The Brew House suggests that people with high blood pressure take a bite first.

There will be fresh "low sugar" fruits as dessert for diabetics, but the restaurant cannot supply "no sugar deserts." Sorry!

Did I miss anything?

Joan

COMPANY MEMO

FROM: Joan Smith

TO: All F****ing Employees

DATE: November 5, 2012

SUBJECT: The F***ing Holiday Party

I've had it with you vegetarian pricks! We're going to keep this party at the Brew House whether you like it or not so you can sit quietly at the table furthest from the "grill of death," as you so quaintly put it, and you'll get your f***ing salad bar, including organic tomatoes. But you know tomatoes have feelings, too. They scream when you slice them. I've heard them scream. I'm hearing them scream right NOW!!

The rest of you f***ing weirdoes can kiss my a**. I hope all of you have a rotten holiday!

Drive drunk and die.

The B**ch from H*ll!!

COMPANY MEMO

FROM: Mary Ann Collier, Acting Human Resources Director

TO: All Employees

DATE: November 10, 2012

SUBJECT: Joan Smith and Holiday Party

I'm sure I speak for all of us in wishing Joan Smith a speedy recovery and I'll continue to forward your cards to her.

In the meantime, management has decided to cancel our Holiday Party and give everyone the afternoon of the 22nd of December off with full pay.

Happy Holidays!

Mary Ann Collier

The reflection? All our concerns about being correct in all activities to avoid the unspoken lawsuit can create chronic stress and eventually illness. Accurate? Some folk believe it is possible. The level of the tone in these folk texts takes on more serious connotations. Again, folk texts are never spoken or written in a vacuum. There is meaning here depending on your persuasion.

The second example of the new tone of folkways texts was collected in various forms from St. Louis informants. Some sent it over the Internet. Others printed it and enclosed the text in cards for birthdays or anniversaries or holiday celebrations. The spirit of the message fits the celebrations of the rites of passage, but the tone reflects a stronger meaning. The folk who "pass it on" seem to be seriously purposeful in the dissemination. The example presented is a hybrid of the many variants now being circulated. The message is clear and suggests that no one could disagree with the meaning.

LIFE IS SHORT: WHAT DO YOU BELIEVE?

A birth certificate shows that we were born.

A death certificate shows that we died.

What did we do in between?

I believe . . .

That we don't have to change friends if

We understand that friends change

I believe . . .

That our background and circumstances

May have influenced who we are, but

We are responsible for who we become

I believe . . .

That we are responsible for what

We do, no matter how we feel.

I believe . . .

That sometimes when I'm angry

I have the right to be angry, but that

Doesn't give me the right to be cruel.

I believe . . .

That either you control your attitude

Or it controls you.

I believe . . .

That you should send this

To all the people you

BELIEVE IN!

There are many, many more "chapters" in the form of this lore. The "believe" mantra takes on death and crises and "other" friendships, even the "haves and have not's." And it does it with the same tone.

The polarity of the folk in these two examples is very obvious. Each represents a cultural standard that is not easily discussed but can be reflected conveniently in the lore. Frustration, impatience, and anger are expressed about "societal stupidity" in the "Company Memo," which, it concludes, if not addressed can lead to serious consequences for all of us. Proverbially, our over sensitivity will "drive us all crazy."

The prayerful approach of "believe" is an answer. But is the answer conciliatory? Nostalgic? Romantic? Realistic? Note: The reader is encouraged to pass on the sentiments to friends whom "they believe in," which is a different form of "belief." It appears to be a need for validations, bonding, and integration, which lore can do.

Both of the examples have a different point of view presented in folkways. The current lore, often passed on through the Internet, is filled with examples of either folk genre. There appears to be an undercurrent of "competition," even a "primal scream." The folk want and need to be heard and they use the patterns of acceptable media—company memos and prayers.

Many more examples of these different arguments, presented by combined folk groups, must be collected before a definitive analysis can be made. One thing is certain: The folk will be heard! And then, it is hoped, we will all understand ourselves and our culture in clearer terms.

What lore are you sending or receiving? Is it introspective or instructional? Is it ironic or sarcastic? Does it stereotype? Is it nostalgic? Is it groupthink? Reasoned? Logical? Possible or practical? Think about it!

Peace! And keep you lore alive.

About the Author

Dr. John L. Oldani—Dr. Jack to his students—is a native of St. Louis and the city's unofficial ambassador. With a PhD in American Studies from Saint Louis University, he was a professor for thirty years, primarily at Southern Illinois University at Edwardsville, and visiting professor at the University of Florida, Gainesville, University of California, Berkeley, and University of Zagreb, Croatia. Dr. Jack's passion, study, and mission have been the folklore of St. Louis. He has collected it for decades throughout the region and has taken it with him to other parts of the country, even the world, to validate and verify.

Dr. Oldani has been a regular guest expert on Americana for radio programs in Boston, Chicago, Phoenix, and Los Angeles in addition to 25 years on KMOX (CBS) in St. Louis. He served as the sole writer for Johnny Cash's radio program, "American Folklore," producing 550 scripts. Dr. Oldani has received numerous teaching awards and was inducted into the Great Professor Hall of Fame. He is also the author of *Passing It On: Folklore of St. Louis* (two volumes), *You Did What in the Ditch? Folklore of the American Quilter*, and *Sweetness Preserved: The Story of the Crown Candy Kitchen*. He resides in St. Louis with his wife, Carollee, three children, and their spouses. But his grandchildren, Gemma and Gianna Oldani, Josie and Ceci Hendrickson, and Charlie Oldani are now his subjects of study and give the greatest meaning to his life and new "research." But after all these years of studying folklore, Dr. Oldani has not discovered the folk cure for baldness and is still searching.

If you have folklore that you would like to share with Dr. Jack, please contact him through his website: stlouisfolklore.com.

Index